KEESING'S SPECIAL REPORTS

Revolution in the Philippines? and *Korea: Enduring Division?* are the first titles in this new series of highly topical current affairs reports. Each concentrates on a country or topic in the spotlight of international news. Succinct examination of the main issues puts the subject clearly in focus, while at the same time the books provide the essential historical background in a full and factual account.

Keesing's Special Reports draw on information and expertise from the editorial team of *Keesing's Record of World Events* (formerly *Keesing's Contemporary Archives*), the monthly news reference service with an unrivalled reputation for accuracy and impartiality. *Keesing's* has appeared continuously since 1931 and is published by Longman Group UK Limited on annual subscription. Details of this service, and the associated Keesing's reference books on world affairs, can be obtained from the Promotions Department, Longman Group UK Limited, 6th Floor, Westgate House, The High, Harlow, Essex CM20 1YR, UK.

REVOLUTION IN THE PHILIPPINES?

REVOLUTION IN THE PHILIPPINES?

A KEESING'S SPECIAL REPORTS

Edited by
MARTIN WRIGHT

Contributors: Judith Bell, James Fenton, Siân Kevill,
D. S. Lewis and Martin Wright

StJ

ST. JAMES PRESS
CHICAGO AND LONDON

REVOLUTION IN THE PHILIPPINES?

Published by Longman Group UK Limited,
Westgate House, The High, Harlow, Essex CM20 1YR, UK.
Telephone (0279) 442601
Telex 817484
Facsimile (0279) 444501

Published in the United States and Canada by St James Press,
233 East Ontario St, Chicago 60611, Illinois, U.S.A.

ISBN 0-582-02628-8   (Longman)
      1-55862-003-6   (St James)

First published in 1988

British Library Cataloguing in Publication Data
Revolution in the Philippines?——(A Keesing's special report).
   1. Philippines. Political events, 1945–1987
   I. Wright, Martin, *1958*–   II. Bell, Judith
   III. Kevill, Siân   IV. Series
   959.9′04

   ISBN 0-582-02628-8

Typesetting by Quorn Selective Repro Ltd,
Queens Road, Loughborough, Leicestershire
Printed and bound in Great Britain by
Biddles Ltd, Guildford and King's Lynn

CONTENTS

Acknowledgements The front cover photographs were provided by Popperfoto and the map on page viii by CARPRESS International Press Agency; permission for their use is gratefully acknowledged. The photographs in the text are by, and remain the copyright of, the editor, Martin Wright.

PREFACE

The turbulent events of February 1986 kept the Philippines constantly in the spotlight of world attention. That month ended in triumph for Cory Aquino, and witnessed the mobilization of "people power" to shield her supporters from the military force of the faltering Marcos machine. The fall of Marcos was now linked in the public mind with the symbol of those yellow-clad demonstrators. But his regime had apparently begun to come unstuck 2½ years earlier, with another dramatic episode: Benigno Aquino gunned down on the steps of the plane that had brought him home. His killing, a crime that would not be explained away, became itself a kind of symbol for charges of corruption and violence levelled at the years of Marcos rule.

Behind these symbolic events and dramatic changes lie profound questions for the Philippines today. This Special Report not only describes the events, it puts them in context—first of all, in Part One, in their historical context, and then, in Part Two in the context of major issues still far from being resolved. The question mark in the title, *Revolution in the Philippines?*, could be read as a question mark against the survival of the new regime, although Cory Aquino has weathered more than two years in office as of the time of this publication. Still on the agenda, however, are challenges to which the Marcos regime had found no constructive response—poverty, the communist insurgency, and separatism in the Moslem south.

The chapters of Part Two look at these matters, issue by issue, and at the relationship with the USA as the Philippines' key ally in the regional power system. Part Two concludes with descriptions of facets of Filipino life; three of these pieces, by James Fenton, have already been published in *The Independent*, and thanks are due to that newspaper for permission to reproduce them here.

Part Three covers reference data on economic and political structure and activity. This book thus becomes not merely a topical briefing but a working tool for researchers and readers seeking a full understanding of the Philippines today.

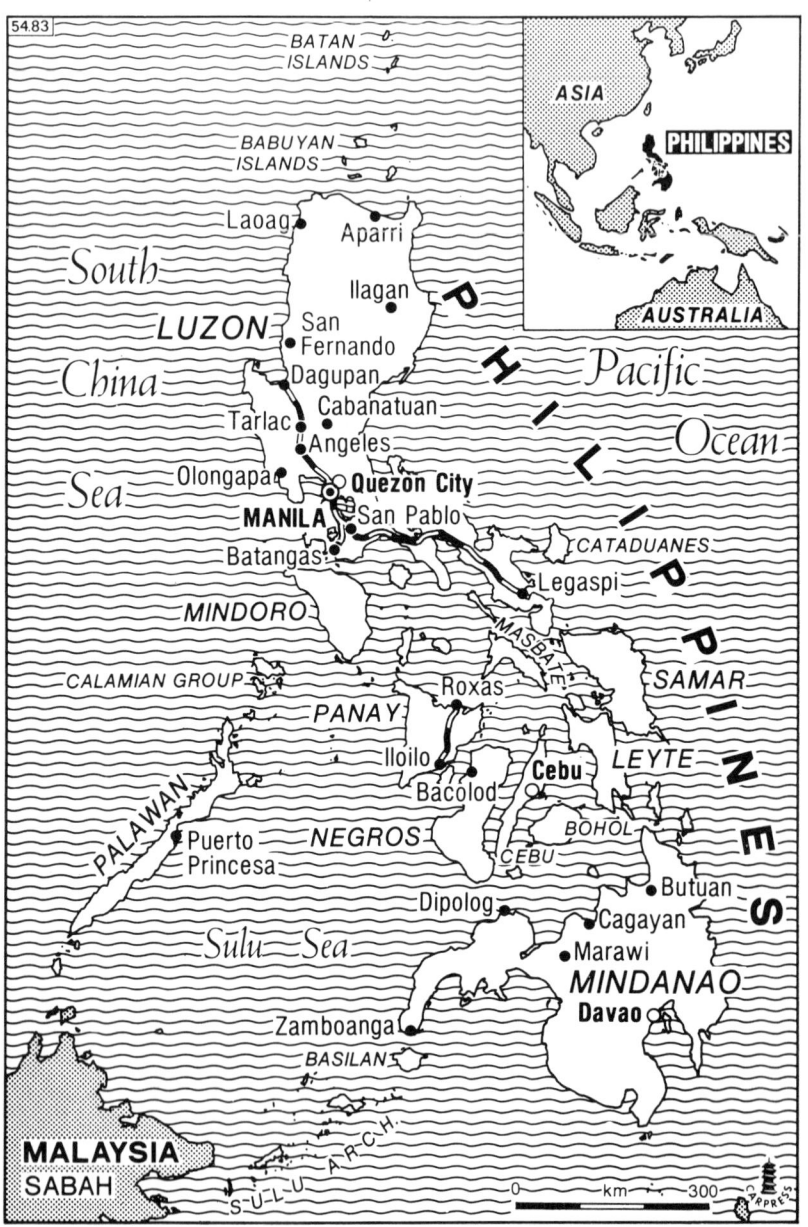

viii

PART ONE

BEFORE PEOPLE POWER: THE PHILIPPINES FROM 1500 TO 1986

Prior to Spanish conquest in the sixteenth century, the 7,000 or so islands which today comprise the Republic of the Philippines had no central government and little cultural homogeneity. Unlike many south-east Asian territories, the country had enjoyed no previous period of imperial integrity, and possessed neither written history nor common language.

The common unit of social and economic organization within the islands' pre-feudalist economy was the *barangay*, a settlement founded upon subsistence agriculture. Most *barangays* were small (consisting of fewer than 500 people) and had little contact with neighbouring settlements. Whilst they contained clear stratifications based on wealth, the social structure of the *barangays* maintained a considerable degree of fluidity. They lacked the rigid, economically-defined class structure of their Spanish conquerors who gradually exerted control over the islands throughout the sixteenth century in the aftermath of Ferdinand Magellan's expedition to Cebu in 1521.

Although the Spaniards were disappointed not to discover reserves of gold or silver, the geographical position of the territory was exploited as a transshipment post on the important trade route between the Far East and the Spanish colonies in Latin America. Under the impact of this lucrative galleon trade the port of Manila, situated on the main island of Luzon, grew rapidly and became the economic centre of the Spanish colony. Elsewhere within the territory local administration was usually in the hands of the Catholic Church which became a substantial landowner upon profits derived from the galleon trade. Under the influence of priests and friars (who in many areas were the sole representatives of the Spanish and who assumed many of the administrative functions of the colonial regime) scattered *barangays* were amalgamated into larger settlements. Some responsibilities were also devolved upon the tradition-al *barangay* rulers who gradually became a native class whose élite position was underpinned by Spanish rule.

Only in the remote northern area of Luzon and in the southern islands of Mindanao and the Sulu archipelago (where Islam had become well

2

established a century before the arrival of the Spanish), was there any sustained resistance to the Spanish conquest. Elsewhere opposition tended to take the form of localized peasant revolts which lacked clear aims and which tended to couch anti-Spanish feeling in religious forms which combined Catholicism with older native religious beliefs.

During the eighteenth century the agricultural potential of the Philippines was developed through the growth of plantations or *haciendas*. This resulted in the rise of a native gentry class (*ilustrados*) which, together with the increasing use of share-cropping as a means of extracting agricultural labour, widened the gap between rich and poor. As Spain declined as an international power during the course of the eighteenth century its hold on the Philippines weakened. The subsequent liberalization of the hitherto restrictive economic policies which had predominated within the territory facilitated an increased penetration by economic interests based in Britain and the USA.

This trend was accelerated dramatically in the mid-nineteenth century through the application of steam power which improved the colony's communications with Europe and made sugar a viable crop. A British entrepreneur, Nicholas Loney, established the first sugar mill on the island of Negros in 1857; over the ensuing years, the island, which had until then been known for its thriving textile industry, was covered with a mass of haciendas set up, often by force, by Loney and local ilustrados from neighbouring islands; by 1900 the island had 274 steam operated mills, while the majority of its population had been reduced to conditions of virtual slave labour on the sugar haciendas.

Heavy capital investment from abroad led to a similar (if less dramatic) transformation in other parts of the colony as land which had previously been used for the production of staple foodstuffs was given over to sugar and later to coconuts. Whilst the production of cash crops led to high profits for the increasingly absentee landowners, the colony as a whole lost its self-sufficiency in the production of food.

While the territory's economic development in conjunction with the decline of Spain had the effect of increasing the disparity in the distribution of wealth it also led to a growing sense of national identity. The articulation of this incipient nationalism was facilitated by educational reforms in 1863 which allowed non-Europeans access to higher education for the first time. Increasingly the *ilustrados* framed reformist demands for a voice in government commensurate with their economic importance. These demands were supported by significant numbers of *Creoles* (those of Spanish descent born in the Philippines) who resented the privileges enjoyed by the *Peninsulares*, Spaniards born in Spain. The first to articulate fully the aspirations of the *ilustrados* was Jose Rizal, whose execution by the Spanish authorities in 1896 ensured that he became a martyr to, and enduring symbol of, Filipino nationalism.

REVOLUTION IN THE PHILIPPINES?

In 1896 Andres Bonifacio founded a revolutionary movement known as *Katipunan* which demanded outright independence for the Philippines. Although Bonifacio fled the country after an attempt by the Spanish to arrest him, the movement grew rapidly under the leadership of Emilio Aguinaldo who became head of a self-styled revolutionary government. The Spanish authorities lacked the capacity to suppress the rebels and eventually paid Aguinaldo and his followers to end their "war of national liberation" and to go into exile. With the outbreak of the Spanish-American war a few months later, Aguinaldo returned with US support and proclaimed Philippine independence on June 12, 1898.

Under the terms of the Treaty of Paris (which was signed in 1898 following the defeat of Spain), the Philippines was ceded to the USA in return for a payment of US$20,000,000. Aguinaldo's relationship with the US forces of occupation and the *ilustrados*-dominated government which they had sponsored, however, rapidly deteriorated into open warfare as he personified the demand for complete independence. Even after his capture in March 1901, sporadic resistance to the US occupation continued.

Under the US administration (which was considerably more enlightened than its predecessor) English was introduced into the education system as the principal medium of instruction as part of a general dissemination of American values and culture. An increasing degree of internal self-government was granted to the colony, with a gradual extension of the franchise from 1907 onwards. The political process remained under the control of the *ilustrados*, however, and the Nationalist Party (established in 1907) dominated all others. Favourable concessions to the agrarian sector (including the under-taxation of land and the exemption from tax of agricultural products) resulted in further land accumulation and the consequent growth in the number of landless peasants. The lingering desire for independence combined with such economic factors served to fuel peasant unrest throughout the 1920s. In a parallel development in urban areas there was a growth in unionization and increasing militancy on the part of the labour movement; the Communist Party of the Philippines (*Partido Komunista ng Philipinas*— PKP) was founded in 1930.

Tax revenues failed to offset the cost of the colony's administration, however, and its economic burden on the USA was exacerbated by an uneven trade balance, with large quantities of Filipino agricultural produce entering the USA under preferential terms, set against a much more limited export of US-manufactured items to the colony. During the 1920s, US agricultural interests and the Federation of Labor lobbied for the granting of full independence for the territory in order that a greater degree of control could be exercised over both Filipino exports to the USA and immigrant labour from the territory which was undermining

4

US wage rates. This perspective was sharpened in the early 1930s by the prolonged US economic depression and the attendant clamour for increased protection for the severely depressed agricultural sector. On November 15, 1935, the Commonwealth of the Philippines was established under the Presidency of Manuel Quezon. The move, which resulted from an Act which had been ratified by President Roosevelt in March 1934, was designed as a transitionary stage with full independence to follow within 10 years. The outbreak of the Pacific War in December 1941 upset this calculation.

The Philippines under Japanese occupation

On December 7, the same day as the Japanese attack on the US naval base at Pearl Harbour, the Imperial Japanese Airforce destroyed the US aircraft base at Clark Field on Luzon. Shortly afterwards the territory was invaded by Japanese troops. General MacArthur, the commander of a combined US and Filipino army of 50,000 men, retreated to the Bataan peninsula and to the fortified island of Corregidor in Manila Bay where his troops were besieged. The defenders of the peninsular surrendered on April 9, 1942, and were joined in captivity on May 6 by the garrison of Corregidor. Before the last rites of this disaster had been enacted, however, both MacArthur and Quezon had escaped abroad to safety.

There followed a period of harsh occupation whereby the territory was subjected to a form of colonial exploitation based upon Japan's military needs and the autarchic aims of its Greater East Asia Co-Prosperity Sphere, which foresaw economic self-sufficiency for Japanese-dominated countries in the region. The resulting constriction of domestic consumption led to severe shortages of essential goods for the civilian population. This, combined with the attitudes of racial superiority displayed by their conquerors and the brutalities of the occupation (not least the conscription of labour), fostered the growth of pro-American sentiments amongst many of the population who saw the USA as a potential liberator.

Sections of the political establishment co-operated with the Japanese, however. Jose Vargas (the former executive secretary of Quezon) led a collaborationist goverment, and Senator Benigno Aquino headed an anti-American nationalist movement called *Kalibapi*. Active resistance to the Japanese was in general sporadic and ineffective, with the exception of the *Hukbalahap* movement which operated in central and southern Luzon. The movement was peasant-based and left-wing in orientation. It couched its resistance to the Japanese occupation by emphasizing the inequalities inherent in the colonial structure of the Philippines. In so doing it sought successfully to build upon earlier traditions of peasant revolt and millenarianism which had been present since the Spanish conquest.

From mid-1942 onwards the war began to run in favour of the Allies. Throughout its occupied territories Japan attempted to harness its faltering war effort to the engine of native nationalism and thereby to build genuine popular support. In the Philippines greater efforts were made to present the conquest as a mechanism for the realization of Filipino aspirations for independence. An important practical consequence of this was the encouragement of the use of native languages within the territory in an effort to reduce the dominance of Western values. The culmination of this process was the granting of full independence on October 14, 1943, whereupon the new country immediately became a "voluntary" member of the Greater East Asia Co-Prosperity Sphere. The essence of the country's relationship with Japan remained largely unchanged, however, although Jose Laurel, the new President, did succeed in mollifying some of the more onerous aspects of Japanese rule.

Liberation and independence

US forces invaded the Philippines in October 1944 and in February 1945 Manila was liberated. The Filipino government-in-exile under Sergio Osmena (who had become President following the death of Quezon in August 1944) returned to resume its duties.

The immediate legacy of the Pacific War lay in the enormous physical damage and economic distortion which it had wrought upon the Philippines. The territory's post-war economic reconstruction was dependent upon US aid, but it became quickly apparent that the availability of that aid was to be inextricably tied to the concession of preferential trading rights to the USA. Among these were the provision of advantageous tariff rates for US goods and the granting of parity rights to US citizens in the exploitation of resources and the operation of public utilities within the Philippines. President Osmena made clear his disapproval of this latter provision, which involved amending the constitution in order to grant foreign citizens rights hitherto reserved for Filipinos; he consequently found himself increasingly unpopular with the US authorities. At the Presidential election of April 23, 1946, Osmena was defeated by Manuel Roxas, who had left the Nationalist Party to contest the Presidency as a Liberal. On July 4, 1946, the Philippine Republic was proclaimed as an independent sovereign state with Roxas as its first President.

The Roxas administration was strongly pro-USA and, using dubious political methods to disqualify some of its opponents, succeeded in gaining the 75 per cent Congressional majority necessary to amend the constitution and thereby assure parity rights for US citizens. In the light of the escalating cold war, the Philippines became tied to the foreign policy priorities of the USA. On March 14, 1947, Roxas signed an agreement which gave the USA a 99 year lease upon 23 US military facilities, including the airforce base at Clark Field and the naval installation at Subic Bay, both of which were seen by the US armed forces as vital in the containment of international communism. The bases' residents enjoyed immunity from the criminal justice system of the Philippines. An amnesty was issued to those who had collaborated with the Japanese. Counter-insurgency measures were also implemented against the *Huks* (who had refused to accept the legitimacy of the country's post-war government and had continued their armed struggle). By the early 1950s the *Huk* challenge had been virtually neutralized through a combination of military successes (including the capture of the movement's leadership) and the initiation of a resettlement programme for landless peasants.

In April 1948 Roxas died and was succeeded by his Vice-President Elpidio Quirino. At the presidential election of 1949 he defeated Jose Laurel amidst numerous accusations of fraud and corruption. Despite the continuing maldistribution of wealth, the Philippines remained comparatively stable throughout the 1950s, thanks to a steady expansion of the middle class, an independent judiciary (which upheld the country's constitution), a press which displayed considerable diversity in political affiliation and a professional army which lacked political ambitions.

In the 1953 presidential elections Quirino was defeated by his former Defence Minister, Ramon Magsaysay, who had left the Liberals to contest the Presidency as the representative of the Nationalist Party. As President he continued the pro-US policies of his predecessors. He was one of the first heads of state to extend diplomatic recognition to South Vietnam and was one of the foremost advocates of the establishment of the South East Asia Treaty Organization (SEATO). Shortly before the presidential election of 1957 he was killed in an aircrash and was was succeeded by his Vice-President, Carlos Garcia who was subsequently elected President.

The Liberals recaptured the Presidency in 1961 when Garcia was defeated by Diosdado Macapagal. Exchange controls were dismantled in return for US stabilization loans, which were conditional on the devaluation of the peso and other concessions to bilateral trade. The continuing rise in the Philippines' balance of payments deficit with the USA, however, necessitated further loans. The effect of the devaluation upon the country's embryonic industrial sector was particularly damaging and caused widespread bankruptcies with many manufacturing enterprises being purchased cheaply by US entrepreneurs.

In the presidential elections of November 9, 1965, Macapagal was defeated by Ferdinand Marcos who had left the Liberals a year earlier and who contested the elections as the Nationalist candidate. Marcos, like his predecessors, proved a staunch ally of the USA. In October 1966 he hosted a seven country "summit conference" at the Malacanang Palace in Manila, which was attended by President Lyndon Johnson of the USA, and which stated its unequivocal support for US policy towards South Vietnam. A month earlier the first detachment of a Filipino expeditionary force of 2,000 men had arrived in South Vietnam.

Despite a deterioration in the overall performance of the economy and a rapidly rising rate of inflation, Marcos broke the traditional pattern of one-term presidents by defeating the challenge of Sergio Osmena in the presidential elections of November 1969. The campaign, like that of 1965, was characterized by a high degree of political violence. The *New York Times* described the election as "the most disputed and acrimonious in the Philippines' history", with the Liberals claiming that widespread fraud, vote-buying and intimidation of candidates and voters had invalidated the result.

On December 31, the day after his inauguration for a second term, Marcos announced that he and his wife Imelda had transferred all of their material possessions to the Ferdinand Marcos Foundation for the promotion of education, science and the arts. Marcos explained the extravagant gesture as an attempt to "set the example of self-denial and self-sacrifice", in order to overcome the country's economic difficulties which were becoming increasingly manifest through shortages in staple foodstuffs such as rice. On February 21, 1970, the peso was floated, leading to an immediate fall of 30 per cent in its value against the US dollar. Despite this and the willingness of the Marcos regime to borrow heavily from the International Monetary Fund, the economic problems of the country continued to intensify.

Rising prices and endemic corruption led to repeated demonstrations and strikes in Manila and other major cities in early 1970. The growing street violence was only controlled by increased use of force by the Army and police. Opposition to the Marcos regime was co-ordinated by the Movement for a Democratic Philippines (MDP) which embraced workers' and students' organizations. The country's subordinate relationship with the USA was also the focus of resentment among the anti-Marcos elements. Demonstrations were held to demand the inclusion of independent figures in the Constitutional Convention (which was due to begin drafting a new constitution in 1971 to replace that drawn up in 1935) and to ensure that Marcos would not attempt to serve a third term as President. Although Marcos offered assurances that he had no such ambition, the demonstrations continued, and both the Malacanang Palace and the US embassy in Manila were the focus of populist attacks.

The Marcos government also faced increasing opposition from the New People's Army (NPA), the military wing of the banned Maoist Communist Party of the Philippines (CPP-ML), which had broken from the pro-Soviet PKP in 1968. By the early 1970s the NPA had succeeded in constructing an effective guerrilla organisation upon the foundations of the *Huk* movement, advocating wholesale land reform and a programme of social justice as the solution to traditional peasant grievances. By 1972 the NPA was acknowledged to be the *de facto* administration in numerous remote areas of the country including parts of Luzon and on several outlying islands, where it undertook land redistribution and raised revenue through the collection of rents and taxes. A series of bombs which exploded in Manila in 1972 were also attributed to NPA sympathizers.

A further challenge to the authority of central government arose in the form of the activities of the Moro National Liberation Front (MNLF) which was established in 1968 as the vehicle for achieving independence or autonomy for the Moslem population of the Philippines. According to the 1970 census returns there were 2,100,000 Moslems (out of a total population of 38,000,000), most of whom were concentrated in the southern provinces of Mindanao where they represented a culturally homogeneous and distinctive group which suffered levels of social and economic deprivation greater than that of their Christian neighbours. By 1971 it was estimated that some 800,000 Moslems were refugees having been evicted from their lands by Christians, and almost 2,000 people had been killed over an 18-month period in the regular fighting which had occurred between armed groups from the two communities. Atrocities perpetrated against Moslem civilians by the Filipino army led to accusations of attempted genocide made against the Marcos government by Libya and other Islamic countries.

Imposition of martial law

The campaign for the legislative elections of November 1971, in which the Liberals achieved considerable gains, was marred by widespread violence. Between August and December the right of *habeas corpus* was suspended in many parts of the country, and Marcos threatened that full martial law might be imposed if the situation did not improve. In addition to the general lawlessness and politically-motivated violence in Manila, the NPA was seen as an increasing threat, with both the government and senior army leaders repeatedly emphasizing the danger of an imminent communist take-over of the government.

On September 23, 1972, Marcos used his emergency powers to decree a state of full martial law throughout the country. Under the decree military commanders in the provinces were ordered to assume those powers hitherto exercised by elected governors and mayors. Most newspapers and radio stations were forced to close and a curfew from midnight to 4 a.m. was imposed. Benigno Aquino, the secretary general of the Liberal Party, was arrested, as were many other prominent members of the opposition and journalists who were associated with publications known to be critical of the Marcos administration. The government also took control of public services such as electricity supplies in Manila, railways and civil aviation, and prohibited strikes in the energy, financial, distributive and educational sectors of the economy.

In an address to the nation the President explained his action on the grounds that "our democracy . . .is endangered by the peril of violent overthrow". The imposition of martial law, he explained, would enable the government to undertake a major drive against the rebels and their supporters, whilst also facilitating measures to reduce the degree of popular dissatisfaction within the country. Such measures he suggested would include "a clean-up of corrupt and sterile government officials", the initiation of land reform, the punishment of those members of the military who had committed offences against the civilian population and a radical reduction of the level of violence which had become endemic to Filipino society.

In the ensuing weeks measures were undertaken towards the realization of these aims. All firearms in the hands of manufacturers, retailers or private citizens were ordered to be handed over to the constabulary, and the carrying of any offensive weapon was prohibited. Several prominent national figures were arrested on charges of maintaining private armies, whilst other citizens were detained for illegally trafficking in weapons. On October 2, Marcos imposed the death penalty for any murder commited with firearms and imprisonment for 20 years or life for killings with other weapons.

Schools and colleges were temporarily closed on September 28 to enable the authorities to remove suspected communists from amongst the staff and students. Some newspapers and radio stations were allowed to reopen on condition that they observed strict government guidelines which dictated that only "correct and objective information on positive national achievements" was to be printed, and must appear without comment or opinion. The country's information media had in the past, claimed Marcos, participated "consciously or unconsciously" in the "communist conspiracy" which had necessitated the imposition of martial law. In an attempt to prevent the recurrence of this situation the government established a press consultative council to provide "self-regulation" for the mass media. It also adopted a system of issuing licenses to those newspapers, radio and television stations which had been permitted to reopen, which had to be renewed on a six-monthly basis and without which they were forbidden to operate. Strict censorship was also imposed upon the film industry in order to prevent the depiction of crime, sex, violence or revolutionary themes.

In an effort to reduce the incidence of corruption Marcos demanded on September 29 that all 400,000 government employees should submit their resignations by October 15 so that the administration could decide, under new civil service regulations, which employees should not be reappointed. Several members of the judiciary and officers of the armed forces were also dismissed and arrested on charges of corruption.

In a decree issued on September 26 Marcos announced the initiation of a comprehensive land reform programme which was aimed at achieving "a dignified existence for small farmers, free from the pernicious institutional restraints and practices which have not only retarded the agriculture of the country but have also produced widespread discontent and unrest amongst our farmers, one of the causes of the existing national emergency". Little serious attempt was made to implement the terms of the programme, however, and the problems arising from the unequal ownership of land remained unresolved and largely unaddressed.

On November 29, 1972, the Constitutional Convention completed almost 18 months of deliberations and approved a new draft constitution containing both long term and transitional provisions. Amongst the former it called for the replacement of the current system of presidential government with a Cabinet system headed by a Prime Minister elected by and responsible to a unicameral legislature. The document called for measures to "philippinize" the country but also recommended the encouragement of foreign investment and the development of joint projects. Amongst the transitional proposals were the creation of an interim legislature pending the election of the new National Assembly, and the confirmation of wide executive powers for the President who would head the government until the new constitution became fully operative.

Upon receipt of the draft constitution Marcos announced that the document would be offered for popular approval in a referendum in January 1973. The provisions of martial law were relaxed to allow limited public debate of the proposals, but in early January 1973 it was announced that the referendum had been postponed indefinitely and the full rigours of martial law were reimposed. Under a further presidential decree, Citizens' Assemblies (called *barangays* in a conscious echo of the pre-colonial era) were established throughout the country and Marcos later claimed that they had endorsed the proposals within the draft constitution. These assemblies were also used to provide the membership of a 4,600 strong "Popular Congress", before which Marcos announced the ratification of the new constitution on January 17. He stated that he had postponed indefinitely the convening of the interim legislature, that elections would be suspended for at least seven years and that martial law would remain in force for as long as was deemed necessary. The only concession to democracy was to be the continued operation of the Citizens' Assemblies.

Attempts to challenge the legality of Marcos' actions were dismissed by the Supreme Court, and on July 27-28 a referendum was held which gave Marcos a mandate "to remain in office beyond 1973 and to complete the reforms which he has initiated under martial law". Voting was compulsory for all citizens over the age of 15 years and, whilst the government committed considerable resources towards achieving a vote in favour, those who opposed the proposition were effectively prevented from campaigning freely. According to the final figures issued by the government on August 3, a total of 18,052,016 votes (over 90 per cent of those cast) had been in favour of the continuation of the personal rule of Marcos. A further referendum held on February 27, 1975, produced another large majority in favour of the retention of martial law.

New regulations relating to the conduct of industrial relations were issued in late 1975 under which strikes and lockouts were prohibited and foreigners were forbidden to participate in labour protests. Nevertheless stoppages took place in early 1976 leading to the arrest of several hundred trade unionists. A further cause of unrest was the decision of Mrs Marcos (the newly appointed governor of Metro Manila) to demolish the shelters of several thousand squatters in and around the capital because of the aesthetic unacceptability of their dwellings.

In August 1976 Marcos announced that the national assembly proposed by the 1973 constitution would not be convened. A further referendum was held in October which again expressed support for a continuation of martial law. It also approved a series of amendments to the 1973 constitution which included the provision of an interim 120 member constituent assembly (*Batasang Pambansa*), some of whose members would be elected and some appointed by the President. It confirmed the right of Marcos to continue to legislate by decree even after the lifting of martial law in the event of an emergency being threatened or of the legislature being "unable to act adequately". A fourth referendum was held in December 1977 in a further attempt to provide some legitimacy derived through popular endorsement for the continuation of the Marcos dictatorship.

When elections for the 200-member *Batasang Pambansa* were finally held in April 1978 the recently created New Society Movement (*Kilusan Bagong Lipunan*—KBL), led by Marcos, won 152 of the 165 elected seats.

Although the martial law prohibition on political parties had been lifted in January, prior to the voting, the government was accused of intimidating opposition candidates and voters and of engaging in fraudulent voting and counting practices. The opposition People's Power Movement (*Lakas Ng Bayan*, known by the acronym *Laban*, which means "fight"), led by the imprisoned former Liberal Senator Benigno Aquino, lost all of the seats which it contested.

When the newly elected assembly convened in June 1978 Marcos accepted the post of Prime Minister in addition to that of President. His new Cabinet included his wife Imelda who, in addition to her post as Governor of Metro Manila, became Minister for Ecology and Human Settlements. Marcos promised to use sparingly his power to legislate by decree, but stated that martial law would remain in force until the new legislature could show the world that "it is as effective if not better than the crisis government".

Although some peripheral aspects of martial law were relaxed, the essence of the dictatorial system established by Marcos continued unaltered and the regime's record on human rights continued to draw international condemnation. Detainees were denied fair trials and torture was used routinely in the extraction of confessions. Aquino, who had been incarcerated since 1972, was eventually arraigned on fabricated charges of murder and of having aided the communists. He was sentenced to death by a military tribunal in November 1977, but international pressure from the USA and elsewhere led to a suspension of the sentence. In December 1979, Benigno Aquino was transferred from prison to his home where he was placed under house arrest.

The Philippines remained dominated by the economic and foreign policy interests of the USA, although in January 1979 concessions were made to Filipino nationalism through the revision of the agreement covering US bases. The 1947 treaty (which had been amended in 1966) was not due to expire until 1991, but Marcos had been attempting to secure an improvement in its terms since the mid-1970s. Under the revised agreement the area covered by the bases was reduced and the economic and military assistance offered in remuneration was increased. The principle of Filipino sovereignty was reaffirmed and several symbolic concessions were made towards it such as the appointment of Filipino base commanders. It was also agreed to renegotiate the terms under which the bases were held at least every five years. A new agreement was concluded on May 31, 1983, for another five years effective from October 1984, which again increased US economic and military assistance.

Marcos extended his grip on the country in January 1980 when the KBL won most of the seats at stake in the first elections for local, regional and provincial offices since 1971. Both *Laban* and the Liberal Party boycotted the elections in protest over the continuation of martial law, although the Nationalist Party did succeed in winning some of the posts.

The problem of guerrilla insurgency remained unreconciled, however, as the government found itself unable to defeat the rebels militarily or to achieve peace through the negotiation of a political settlement. Marcos had attempted to pursue the latter strategy in relation to the MNLF on several occasions following increasing international pressure from the Islamic Conference Organization (ICO) which in 1973 had demanded a revision of the government's policy towards the Moslem population. Cosmetic changes were made in the form of concessions towards the provision of greater Moslem educational and cultural facilities, but the fighting continued on a sporadic basis interspersed with selective amnesties for those rebels who were prepared to surrender their weapons.

In January 1975 talks between representatives of the Marcos government and the MNLF were held in Jeddah, Saudi Arabia, under the auspices of the ICO but broke down because of the government's refusal to countenance any significant autonomy for the southern provinces. In an attempt to undercut the MNLF's support, the government engaged in talks with other Moslem organizations in mid-1975. Once again although minor concessions were agreed, they were insufficient to bring an end to the fighting.

Renewed ICO-sponsored talks between the rebels and the government, which were held in Tripoli, Libya, in December 1976 resulted in agreement on a ceasefire in return for the the granting of autonomy to the 13 provinces comprising Mindanao, the Sulu archipelago and Palawan Island. The agreement foundered upon the later insistence by the government that referenda should be held in the affected provinces. Talks were renewed in February 1977 but broke down as each side sought to revise the terms of the autonomy agreement and the territory to which it was to be applied. Nevertheless, on March 26, the government declared the 13 provinces as an autonomous region and began creating the basis of a regional administrative structure. A referendum was held on April 17, despite the MNLF's refusal to participate on the grounds that no such measure had been included in the original Tripoli agreement. According to the government's figures, 75 per cent of the electorate participated in the poll and 93.9 per cent of votes were cast against the autonomy proposals. Despite the referendum results, the embryonic regional government remained in place (under the terms of a law of February 1977 which had theoretically divided the whole country into 12 autonomous regions) but the MNLF refused to participate within it and was reported to have reverted to its original demand for total independence.

The ceasefire of December 1976 gradually broke down during the course of 1977 although both sides refrained from mounting major offensive operations. The war continued thereafter on a sporadic basis.

By the early 1980s the government claimed to have effectively neutralized the threat posed by the MNLF, although when martial law was lifted elsewhere in the country in 1981, it was retained in the Moslem provinces. The military capacity of the guerrillas was certainly retarded by the opening of severe internal divisions resulting from ideological and personal differences which were aggravated by the efforts of the ICO to persuade the movement's leadership to accept a form of autonomy rather than continuing to press for complete independence. By late 1982 three distinct groupings had emerged—(i) the main MNLF faction led by Nur Misuari and supported initially by Libya and thereafter by Iran; (ii) the Moslem Islamic Liberation Front (MILF) led by Hashim Salamat and supported by Egypt; (iii) the smaller Bangsa Moro National Liberation Front (BMNLF) led by Dimas Pundato and supported by Saudi Arabia.

While the problem posed by Moslem insurgency remained comparatively stable during the final decade of the Marcos regime, the threat which originated from the NPA increased dramatically over the same period. In September 1971 a Senate Committee had estimated that the NPA numbered only 350 men and presented "no military threat". Yet by 1981 it was estimated that the organization had in excess of 10,000 fighters and was functioning as an unofficial government in many areas of the country. It was also conducting an increasingly effective "liquidation campaign" against representatives of local government.

In response to the growth of the movement and to the popularity of its policies of land reform and social justice in many rural areas, the government was forced to alter its strategy in 1981. Instead of pursuing the policy of sporadic (and largely ineffective) military operations combined with selective amnesties, it attempted to apply the "strategic hamlet" concept which had been used by the British to combat insurgency in Malaya in the 1950s, and later by the USA in Vietnam. The programme sought to deprive the guerrillas of their mass base by shifting up to 250,000 peasants and relocating them within hamlets guarded by army units. The policy was incompetently administered, however, and the injustices and disruption which were endemic upon its implementation often had the effect of increasing anti-government sentiments amongst the people.

The post martial law period 1981-1985

In a nationwide broadcast on January 17, 1981, Marcos announced the lifting of martial law in all but the southernmost provinces of the country. Legislative power was formally transferred to the interim National Assembly elected in April 1978, and it was confirmed that elections to a

15

permanent Assembly would be held in 1984. The President retained potentially wide powers, however, under a new National Security Code and Public Safety Act which empowered him to order arrests, to close media outlets and to suspend the right of *habeas corpus* "whenever in his judgement there exists a grave emergency". Marcos also announced that the first presidential election since 1969 would be held later in the year.

Further constitutional amendments were agreed by referendum in April 1981 and provided for the President to be popularly elected rather than being chosen by the National Assembly. Once elected, a President would serve a six-year term and would be eligible to seek re-election for an unlimited number of terms thereafter. As the head of state the President would nominate a Prime Minister who would be answerable both to him and to the legislature.

The presidential election was held in June 1981, with Marcos standing as the official KBL candidate. It was boycotted by the main parties of the opposition. Senator Benigno Aquino (who had remained in the USA since being permitted to travel there in 1980 for medical treatment) condemned the proceedings as a publicity stunt, the outcome of which had already been determined. A total of 12 candidates did oppose Marcos, however, including nominees from rival wings of the Nationalist Party. Amid allegations of widespread malpractice and fraud concerning both the campaign and the count, Marcos was declared to have been elected with 88 per cent of the votes cast. He duly began a new six-year term of office on June 30, 1981.

The re-election of Marcos was an important catalyst in accelerating the movement towards unity on the part of his opponents. In February 1982 the United Nationalist Democratic Organization (Unido) was established as an anti-Marcos alliance. It included *Laban*, the Nationalist Party, and the United Democratic Opposition, an eight-party coalition led by Salvador Laurel and grouped around the Liberal Party. Although the movement was led within the Philippines by Laurel, it was Aquino who was widely recognized as its most charismatic and influential figure. In mid-1983 he decided to return to the Philippines despite warnings by the government that he would be subject to renewed arrest and rumours of plots against his life. He arrived at Manila airport on August 21 and was shot dead on the tarmac as he stepped from the airliner. During the 10-day mourning period which followed Aquino's death it was estimated that over 2,000,000 people paid their last respects to the murdered man.

The official version of the assassination maintained that Aquino had been killed by Rolando Galman, a communist assassin, who in turn had been shot dead immediately by troops. From the start, however, there were inconsistencies in the official version of events and it was widely suspected that the crime had been committed with the connivance of members of the armed forces or the government. A commission of inquiry into Aquino's death was established in late 1983 under Corazon Agrava, a former appeal court judge. Testimony from eye witnesses suggested that Aquino had been shot in the back of the head from point blank range as he descended the stairway, the angle being such that it was impossible for Galman (who was standing some distance away) to have fired the shot.

The manner of Aquino's death served to galvanize the opposition and widespread popular unrest followed with repeated calls for the resignation of Marcos and the restoration of full democratic rule. Frequent demonstrations occurred throughout the remainder of the year with middle-class support for the protesters much in evidence. In January 1984 the principal parties of the opposition, consisting of Unido and the newly-formed "Compact Alliance", announced their intention to boycott legislative elections scheduled for May unless a serious programme of democratic reforms was initiated. The Compact Alliance consisted of opposition groups which had rejected Unido's policy of non-cooperation with the left and its unequivocal support for the continued presence of the US bases. Foremost amongst these was PDP-*Laban* led by Mr Teofisto Guingona, which consisted of an alliance between *Laban* and the Philippine Democratic Party (PDP). After the government announced a number of limited concessions, Unido and PDP-*Laban* agreed to participate in the poll by running joint candidates, despite the refusal of other opposition groups to take part.

The elections were marred by violence and numerous allegations of malpractice and the intimidation of voters by the KBL. Initial reports by the independent National Citizens' Movement for Free Elections (Namfrel) suggested that the opposition was running slightly ahead of the KBL. The official results, however, which emerged after considerable delays, gave the KBL an overwhelming victory. The final distribution of seats within the Assembly increased the opposition's representation from 13 to 55, out of a total of 200, 17 of whom were nominated by the President.

Despite the continuation of anti-government demonstrations the newly elected National Assembly was opened on July 23. Marcos appealed for national unity and promised that martial law would not be reimposed. Once again he refused to relinquish his power to legislate by decree, although he reiterated his earlier promises to use it only in the case of a genuine emergency. The continuing strength of feeling against the Marcos regime was clearly illustrated on August 21, however, when over 1,000,000 people attended a rally in Manila to commemorate the anniversary of Aquino's death.

Although it had been hoped that the elections would restore economic confidence, the country's economy remained in a precarious state, suffering from a substantial flight of capital following the Aquino assassination. There was an alarming growth in the country's foreign debt, whilst the shortage of foreign exchange led to increasing difficulties in financing the import of the raw materials required by industry. The result was the closure of many businesses and a growth in unemployment. In the first of a series of austerity measures designed to combat the country's debt crisis, Marcos used his decree powers on May 17,1984, to increase import duties and to raise indirect taxes on petroleum products. Further monetary and fiscal measures followed in an attempt to reduce imports and to attract foreign capital. Among these were the increases in import duties, cuts in public expenditure, and the floating of the peso which resulted in an immediate *de facto* devaluation of over 22 per cent. The measures also resulted in rapid price rises which in turn fuelled the growing popular opposition to the government.

The conclusions of the Agrava Commission's report, as published in October 1984, exacerbated the regime's problems. Having interviewed over 200 people it concluded that Aquino's death had resulted from a military conspiracy. Although the Commission failed to agree upon the extent to which leading figures had been involved in the crime, its majority report concluded that the murder had resulted from a military conspiracy which had been sanctioned by the Chief of Staff of the Armed Forces, General Fabian Ver. In January 1985, 26 people (including Ver, who was a close confidant of Marcos) were charged with involvement in the crime. In December all were acquitted despite the incriminating evidence against them. Although Ver resumed his duties as Chief of Staff the stigma of the government's suspected complicity in the crime haunted the Marcos regime for the remainder of its existence.

Exploiting the government's unpopularity in the aftermath of the Aquino assassination, the NPA increased both the sphere and scale of its operations throughout 1983 and 1984. The government gradually abandoned its strategic hamlet concept and returned to the policy of local military offensives in NPA-controlled territory, although the increasing demoralization of the army meant that few successes were achieved. The movement also increased its activities in the country's major cities, including Manila, through a concerted campaign of assassinations. These acts, conducted by its "sparrow squads", helped to foster the image of lawlessness and impotence which was rapidly becoming associated with the Marcos administration.

In January 1985, the Defence Minister Juan Ponce Enrile stated that the NPA "constituted the most formidable threat to our national security today and will continue to do so". He estimated that the movement had grown by 23 per cent per annum since 1981, and had been active during 1984 in over 80 per cent of the country's 73 provinces resulting in the death of over 900 soldiers and 1,000 civilians. Although some 1,000 guerrillas had been killed during the course of the campaign, the NPA's front line strength remained upwards of 20,000 fighters.

By early 1985, the political opposition had formed itself into two distinctive groups which together covered almost the entire political spectrum. The first was the conservative-liberal Unido led by Laurel, and the second was a more loosely organized liberal-left grouping within which Corazon Aquino was playing an increasingly prominent role as custodian of the values and reputation of her murdered husband. The two groups continued to be divided on several important policy areas, not least in their attitude to the continued presence of the US military bases of which Unido had been a consistent supporter but which many to the left of Laurel had come to see as inconsistent with real Filipino independence. Despite the differences, however, there was a widespread realization that the most immediate task of removing the Marcos regime was of sufficient importance to subordinate ideological and policy differences to the greater interest of tactical co-operation.

Opposition demonstrations calling for the resignation of Marcos, often supported by leading members of the clergy, became a common feature within Manila. Although contained by riot police using guns, tear-gas and clubs, their cumulative effect was to strip away the few remaining vestiges of legitimacy which the Marcos regime had endeavoured to retain. They symbolized the massive popular disaffection from a regime whose failures could no longer be disguised beneath layers of censorship, propaganda and repression. These failures had become self-evident in the rising prices and corruption which had become endemic to the administration, and which served to highlight its wider economic failures. They had become visible too in the regime's inability to make any significant progress in dealing with the guerrilla struggle being waged by its communist and Moslem opponents. The administration could neither defeat them militarily nor politically through the implementation of the radical structural reforms which could have undercut their appeal and opened the way for a negotiated settlement.

Under growing US pressure to re-establish the basis of some democratic legitimacy for his continued rule, Marcos called a presidential election for early 1986. He was confident that, as in the past, the ruling apparatus at his disposal would be sufficient to pre-determine the result through ballot rigging, the intimidation of voters and opponents alike and the manipulation of the final count. On this occasion, however, the opposition, unified under the widow of the regime's foremost victim, was to achieve through collective action that which Marcos had sought for so long to deny through the ballot box.

THE FALL OF MARCOS

It was during the early hours of November 4, 1985, during a live interview on US television, that President Marcos announced his intention to hold presidential elections. At a political rally in Tarlac province later that day Marcos said that the elections, to be held on January 17, would "erase doubts regarding the popularity of my administration".

The 12-party United Nationalist Democratic Organization (Unido) alliance led by Salvador Laurel pointed out on November 5 that under the constitution a snap election could not take place unless the president became permanently incapacitated, died, resigned or was removed from office. However, after discussions on November 14 between the ruling party Marcos's New Society Movement (KBL—*Kilusan Bagong Lipunan*) and opposition members of the National Assembly, it was agreed to delay the elections for a few weeks. The Assembly on November 26 accordingly approved by 77 votes to 41 a bill which set the presidential and vice-presidential elections for February 7. The Supreme Court confirmed the legitimacy of the elections on December 19, rejecting 11 petitions from opposition politicians contesting their constitutionality.

Late in the evening of December 11, only 90 minutes before the deadline for the filing of nomination papers by election candidates, Aquino and Laurel announced that they had agreed on a joint ticket with the former as the presidential candidate and the latter as the vice-presidential candidate. The unexpected opposition agreement came a few hours after Marcos had caused another surprise by announcing that Arturo Tolentino was to be his vice-presidential running mate. Tolentino, who had a reputation as an independent-minded politician and had occasionally been critical of Marcos's decree-making powers, had been dismissed from his post as Foreign Minister in March 1985 after disagreements with Marcos over Foreign Ministry appointments.

The prospect of a united opposition ticket had suffered an apparent setback in mid-November because of disagreements in the National Alliance Council (NAC—also known as the National Unification Committee or Council), which since its formation at an opposition conference in March had been attempting to organize the selection of a single opposition presidential candidate. A new opposition grouping of

Aquino's supporters emerged on November 18, however, led by the former senators Lorenzo Tanada and Jovito Salonga, and including most of the leadership of the PDP-*Laban* alliance. The new grouping, which was called *Laban ng Bayan* (People's Struggle), or just *Laban*, formally drafted Mrs Aquino as its presidential candidate on December 1.

Aquino had confirmed her intention to stand for the presidency on December 3. She was seen as something of a reluctant candidate who had asked that the signatures of 1,000,000 supporters be collected before she would commit herself as a presidential candidate. She had told a rally of her supporters in Tarlac on November 27 that she had not yet decided if she would stand, although she admitted that she would "never be able to forgive myself if I live with the knowledge that I could have done something and I did not do anything".

Laurel declared on Dec. 8 that he was going to contest the election separately from Aquino; he had offered to be Aquino's vice-presidential running-mate on a Unido ticket, subject to her acceptance of Unido as the nationwide "dominant opposition party", and had rejected her counter--proposal that they both stand as candidates of a Unido-*Laban* "grand coalition", on the grounds that he was unable to "sacrifice my party and my principles". The final agreement reached on December 11, by which Aquino and Laurel agreed to stand together as Unido candidates for the presidency and vice-presidency, followed appeals to them by Cardinal Jaime Sin, the Archbishop of Manila, "to think of the greater interest of the country".

Throughout the election campaign Marcos claimed that Aquino was neither experienced enough nor strong enough to handle the country's economic problems or the communist insurgency, that she was a tool of the communists and had communist advisers, and that an Aquino victory would sooner or later result in communist rule in the Philippines. Aquino, who strongly denied that she had communist associations, responded to the charge of inexperience by admitting that she had no experience "in cheating, stealing, lying and assassinating political opponents"; she promised to "lead by example" and to end the corruption and the injustice which she equated with Marcos's rule. In the course of the campaign Aquino attracted larger and more enthusiastic crowds than Marcos in every part of the country except in traditionally pro-Marcos areas of northern Luzon.

Speaking at a meeting in Baguio (200 miles north of Manila) on January 2, 1986, Aquino said that she would welcome communists into her government if they renounced violence. Observers saw this remark as either a serious misjudgement on her part or a mistake in that she had meant to say that she would welcome communists into the political process in general. On the following day Marcos said that this statement confirmed his charge that Aquino was supported by communists. At a meeting in Manila on January 6 Aquino clarified her position by saying that she would not allow a communist into her cabinet if she were elected President.

The Moslem secessionist problem became an election issue when, on January 13, Marcos accused the opposition of "an act of treason", following a meeting in Spain between Mrs Aquino's brother-in-law, Agapito "Butz" Aquino, and Nur Misuari, the exiled leader of the MNLF (the main Moslem faction fighting for independence in the southern Philippines). Marcos accused Mrs Aquino of signing with the MNLF a "preliminary understanding" on independence in the south. She denied the charge, calling it "a lie", while Butz Aquino also denied that any deal had been signed with the MNLF; he admitted that he had met Misuari, without Mrs Aquino's knowledge, with the aim of restoring peace in Mindanao (the main area of conflict), but added that "peace should never come at the price of dismemberment of the Philippines". Aquino's stated position on the Moslem secessionist issue at this time was that she would fully implement the 1976 Tripoli agreement, signed by a Philippine government representative and Misuari, which granted a degree of autonomy to the Moslem areas in the south.

Unido outlined its "minimum programme" on January 3 setting out measures which would be implemented upon an election victory. Among the measures were (i) repudiation of all arrangements and agreements made by the Marcos administration which were seen to be against the national interest; (ii) amendment of the constitution to ensure "checks and balances" in government; (iii) a guarantee of press freedom; (iv) the elimination of corruption; and (v) the release of all political prisoners. On the issue of US military bases in the Philippines the programme said that Unido would respect the current agreement, which was due to expire in 1991, and would "keep its options open" thereafter. Aquino reiterated this position on the US bases on a number of occasions during the campaign; she was quoted on February 4 as saying that "no sovereign state should allow part of its territory to be under the control of a foreign power for ever".

Aquino outlined her economic policy at a meeting with members of the business community on January 6. She said that she regarded "the private sector as the engine of the economy" and that she was relying on it "to be the prime mover of the effort towards national recovery"; she also promised "an enhanced environment for private initiative", but said that "beyond a certain point, respect for market forces must yield to the demands of conscience". She said that she would "vigorously seek to renegotiate the terms of our foreign debt", adding that "our economy cannot possibly endure, nor our people long accept, a situation where nearly half of our export earnings must go to interest payments alone, and for loans that have benefited only a favoured few".

THE FALL OF MARCOS

The Maoist Communist Party of the Philippines (CPP-ML) announced on January 6 that it was boycotting the forthcoming elections. The Japanese news agency Kyodo reported on January 9 that a leader of the NPA had confirmed that his organization would also be advocating a boycott, and would not support Aquino because she was "representing landowners and capitalists". The left-wing *Bagong Alyamsang Makabayan* (New Nationalist Alliance, more commonly known as *Bayan*), established in March 1985, announced on January 8 that it too was boycotting the elections. Among other left-wing groups calling for a boycott were the National Democratic Front (NDF, an illegal CPP-organized grouping of leftist bodies), which described the election as "American-inspired", and the *Kilusang Mayo Uno* ("May 1st Movement") trade union group.

A total of 51 people were killed in election-related incidents during the period up to February 6. The NPA honoured its pledge not to interfere in the campaign, however, and the majority of those who died were opposition supporters. At least 26 people were killed in violent incidents on election day itself. The National Citizens' Movement for Free Elections (Namfrel, an independent electoral monitoring organization) reported many irregularities and acts of violence throughout the country; one Namfrel member was shot dead while attempting to guard ballot boxes.

Jose Concepcion Jr, the chairman of Namfrel, had told members of the group on February 2 to "guard every step of the electoral process", and, if necessary, to chain themselves to ballot boxes to prevent people stealing or tampering with them. However, Namfrel was unable to prevent the removal of names from the electoral list before the election day; many supporters of Aquino complained of this and Concepcion later estimated that about 400,000 people in Metro Manila (10 per cent of the electorate) had been disenfranchised in this way. Other types of electoral fraud were reported over a wide area, and there was also evidence of widespread intimidation, harassment and violence. Observers reported that most infringements and acts of intimidation or violence appeared to have been carried out by supporters of President Marcos.

A 20-member US delegation of observers, sent by President Reagan and led by Richard Lugar, a Republican Senator and the chairman of the Senate foreign relations committee, arrived in Manila on February 5. Lugar said after the poll that he was "deeply disturbed" by some of the events of February 7. Members of a second, unofficial, international observer group were banned from polling stations, as were journalists and other foreigners.

Early in the morning of February 8 both Marcos and Aquino were predicting victory, but the count soon became slow and confused; the longer the official National Committee on Elections (Comelec) took to count the vote, the more the opposition became convinced that further fraud was being carried out. This suspicion was confirmed by a group of computer operators at the Comelec headquarters, who resigned in protest on February 9 after they had complained of discrepancies between the voting figures which they were putting into the computer and the total figures which later emerged. Some of the 30 women who resigned said that by their calculations Aquino was ahead in the count, but the published totals were showing a lead for Marcos.

A conference of about 50 Roman Catholic bishops issued a statement on February 14 denouncing the election as unparalleled in fraudulence and as "pointing to a criminal use of power to thwart the sovereign will of the people".

The National Assembly began checking election returns on February 10. Although a period of 30 days was allowed before the Assembly was required to declare the results, the KBL ignored opposition demands for an investigation into the numerous alleged irregularities, and on February 15 the (KBL-dominated) Assembly proclaimed the re-election of Marcos as President.

Under the electoral system both Comelec and Namfrel were to check the returns, which were then passed on to the National Assembly where the result was confirmed and formally declared. According to Comelec's final figures Marcos received 10,807,197 votes and Aquino received 9,291,761. However, according to Namfrel, which had only counted 69 per cent of the returns at this time, Aquino had received 7,502,601 votes and Marcos 6,787,566.

Aquino told a rally of several hundred thousand people in Manila on February 16 that she would launch a national strike and campaign of "active resistance by peaceful means" in protest at Marcos's "victory", and that the campaign would continue until the Marcos regime was brought down.

In his first comment on the elections President Reagan said on February 10 that the result showed that there was a strong two-party system in the Philippines, and that the two sides would have to come together "to make the government work". On the following day Reagan had talks with Lugar and later told correspondents that although Lugar had reported "the appearance of fraud" there was "no hard evidence beyond that general appearance"; he also suggested that both sides might have been guilty of electoral fraud. Later on February 11 Reagan announced that he was sending Philip Habib, the President's special envoy to the Middle East from May 1981 to June 1983, as a special envoy to the Philippines, to "assess the desires and needs of the Filipino people". Aquino responded with a statement on February 12 challenging the neutral position adopted by Reagan and advising him to consult his embassy in Manila and the delegation which he had sent to observe the elections. She added: "I would wonder at the motives of a friend of democracy who chose to conspire with Marcos to cheat the Filipino people of their liberation." Aquino also criticized Reagan's suggestion that both sides might have cheated in the election, saying that even Reagan's own observers had found no evidence of opposition fraud.

In a statement issued on February 15, soon after the National Assembly's declaration that Marcos had won the election, Reagan said that although his observers had not yet completed their report "it has already become evident, sadly, that the elections were marred by widespread fraud and violence perpetrated largely by the ruling party". The statement went on to say that the fraud and violence were "so extreme that the election's credibility has been called into question both in the Philippines and in the USA". On the same day Habib arrived in Manila for a seven-day visit and had his first meetings with Marcos, Aquino and Cardinal Sin on February 17. Aquino told Habib that she had no intention of cancelling her non-violent resistance campaign of opposition against Marcos in an effort to force him to resign.

A serious blow was struck against the Marcos regime on February 22 when Juan Ponce Enrile (the Defence Minister) and Lt.-Gen. Fidel Ramos (the Deputy Chief of Staff of the Armed Forces) occupied Camp Aguinaldo, the Defence Ministry headquarters in Manila. They announced that they no longer considered Marcos to be the legitimate president of the Philippines, and that Aquino had been cheated of victory in the election. Both men also said that they had recently learnt that Marcos had been planning to arrest them and to launch a crack-down on the opposition. Later that day Ramos joined troops loyal to him at Camp Crame, the national police headquarters.

In response to a call from Cardinal Sin to protect the rebels, thousands of people, including priests and nuns, expressed their hostility to Marcos by pouring on to the streets to form a protective human shield around the rebel bases. Thus was born the concept of "people power" which was to become the enduring international hallmark of the Aquino revolution. With disregard for the safety of the huge crowds Marcos threatened to "wipe out" Enrile, Ramos and the rebel troops. On February 23, however, Reagan indicated that US aid to the Philippines would be terminated if Marcos used force against the rebels. He later endorsed a statement declaring that "the mandate of the people does no longer belong to the [Marcos] regime", and on the following day called on Marcos to step down, saying that a solution to the crisis "can only be achieved through a peaceful transition to a new government".

About 500 loyal Marcos troops, supported by tanks and armoured personnel carriers, were prevented from launching an attack on Camp Aguinaldo on February 23 by thousands of people blocking the streets. Enrile joined Ramos at Camp Crame later that day. The growing support of the rebels within the armed forces was demonstrated when a helicopter fired a rocket at the presidential palace on February 24 and then destroyed five government helicopters and an aeroplane which were on the ground at Villamor Air Base outside Manila. Rebel soldiers also took control of the main government radio and television networks.

Marcos declared a state of emergency at a press conference on February 24. During the course of the conference Gen. Ver requested firmly that Marcos allow him to use maximum force against the rebels. Apparently wary of alienating those within the US administration who contiued to support him, however, Marcos insisted that Ver should only use light weapons against the rebels, and that his troops should disperse the civilian crowds without opening fire. Some reports suggested that Marcos later ordered mortar attacks on Camp Crame, but that his orders were not obeyed. On the night of February 24-25 a number of people were injured when troops loyal to Marcos opened fire on crowds outside the presidential palace.

Both Marcos and Aquino were formally sworn in as President early on February 25 in ceremonies held in separate parts of the capital. By that evening, however, growing defections to the rebels among members of the armed forces, mass popular opposition and the imminent US recognition of Aquino as President persuaded Marcos that he had to step down and leave the country. Just after 9.00 p.m. two helicopters carrying Marcos, Ver and various family members, took off from Malacanang palace and flew to Clark Air Base. Shortly afterwards jubilant crowds scaled the palace gates and ransacked the private apartments and offices of Marcos while hundreds of thousands of people took to the streets to celebrate the downfall of his regime.

AQUINO'S FIRST YEAR

Upon her inauguration on February 25, 1986, Mrs Aquino appointed her Vice-President, Salvador Laurel, as Prime Minister, with Enrile as Defence Minister and Ramos (who was promoted to full General) as Chief of Staff of the Armed Forces. On the following day Aquino announced her full Cabinet, in which Laurel was given the additional responsibility of the Foreign Affairs portfolio. In addition to leading members of Unido and the *Laban* coalition the Cabinet included Jose Fernandez who was retained as Governor of the Central Bank in the outgoing government.

The main issues confronting the Aquino government at the moment of its inception were (i) the need to dismantle the coercive apparatus of the former regime and to establish for itself a basis of clear constitutional legitimacy; (ii) to contain the counter-revolutionary threats posed by Marcos supporters and disaffected elements within the armed forces; (iii) to attempt to end the insurgency campaigns being waged by the communist New People's Army and the Moslem secessionists; and (iv) to reverse the economic deterioration which had characterized the Philippines in the final years of the Marcos regime.

The quest for constitutional legitimacy

President Aquino began to confront the first of these issues on February 28, when she ordered the release of all of the country's estimated 450 political prisoners. This order was largely complied with although the military was reluctant to release four leading NPA members—Jose Maria Sison, the chairman of the central committee of the CPP, who had been imprisoned at a military base in Manila since 1977; Bernabe Buscayno (alias Commander Dante), the commander-in-chief of the NPA; Alexander Birondo, the leader of an NPA special operations unit; and Ruben Alegre, a member of Birondo's unit which was said to have been responsible for the assassination of a Manila police chief in 1984. These four were all finally released on March 5 after considerable disagreement between those in favour of their liberation (including Aquino) and Enrile and Ramos, who had warned that their release would increase the

27

problem of fighting the insurgency and would discourage the armed forces.

On March 2, Aquino announced the full restoration of the right of *habeas corpus*. By mid-June a total of 519 detainees had been released, but the Task Force on Detainees (a church-based human rights organization) estimated that there were at least a further 596 political prisoners, many of whom were serving sentences after being found guilty of fabricated criminal charges. Many of those released claimed to have suffered torture whilst in detention, and an investigation of such allegations was begun by a seven-member Presidential Commission on Human Rights, established on March 18 under the chairmanship of a former senator, Jose Diokno. This Commission was given wide powers to subpoena witnesses and to consult classified information, in order to inquire into human rights abuses under the previous regime.

In early March the 13 justices of the Supreme Court, all appointed by Marcos, complied with a government request to resign their positions, as did the nine members of Comelec. On March 7 the Information Minister, Teodoro Locsin, announced the abolition of government censorship of newspapers, radio and television. The new government also began the wholesale removal of local office holders and their replacement with government appointees pending the holding of fair local elections.

This dismantling process was continued on March 25, by Aquino's proclamation of a "Freedom Constitution", which empowered her to appoint local and provincial officials and members of the judiciary, and to decree and revoke legislation. The new constitution abolished the unicameral National Assembly which was described by Aquino as a "cancer in our political system", a reference to its domination by the KBL. The post of Prime Minister was also abolished. The new constitution guaranteed the maintenance of all existing individual rights, however, and Aquino promised that a commission would be appointed within 60 days to draft a fresh constitution which would then be submitted to a nationwide referendum for approval.

The proclamation ended several weeks of speculation within the new government as to the most appropriate method through which it could be legitimized. Some Cabinet members had advised the establishment of a "revolutionary government" with powers to sweep aside legal impediments arising from the constitution imposed under martial law by Marcos in 1973, whereas others urged the retention of existing institutions such as the National Assembly to provide the necessary legal endorsement of Aquino's presidency. At her first Cabinet meeting on March 12 Aquino had appointed a five-member committee headed by the Minister of Justice, Neptali Gonzales, to consider the issue. Its report, submitted to the Cabinet on March 19, had recommended the establishment of a revolutionary government, but in her March 25 proclamation Aquino preferred to describe her regime as "provisional"; at a press conference following the announcement Gonzales referred to the constitution as "civilian in character, revolutionary in origin, democratic in essence and transitory in nature".

Opposition to the Assembly's abolition was expressed by several Cabinet Ministers, including Enrile, as well as by Assembly members who called unsuccessfully upon the President to reverse her decision.

On May 25, before a crowd of 100,000 people gathered to celebrate her first three months in office, Aquino announced the creation of a 50-member commission to draft a new constitution. The composition of the Constitutional Commission (Concom) reflected a wide cross-section of Filipino society, although known communists were specifically excluded from amongst the 44 nominees appointed by Aquino. Five seats on the Commission were left vacant "in the spirit of reconciliation" for supporters of Marcos, and one seat was reserved for a nominee from the *Iglesia ni Kristo* church, a small pro-Marcos Christian sect. At its inaugural meeting on June 2 the Commission unanimously chose Cecilia Munoz-Palma, a former Supreme Court justice and a supporter of Aquino, as its president. In a short opening address to Concom Aquino promised not to interfere in its work but exhorted its members to "please be quick" in the execution of their task.

On October 12, after deliberating for a little over four months, Concom approved the final draft of a new constitution by 44 votes to two (four members being absent). President Aquino received the document a a signing ceremony on October 15, and confirmed that it would be the subject of a national referendum to be held on February 2, 1987 and, if accepted, it would then replace the interim "Freedom Constitution".

In addition to a bill of rights guaranteeing a full range of liberal freedoms, the draft constitution provided for a six-year presidential term (including the prohibition of any individual from serving more than a single term), a bicameral legislative Congress consisting of a 250-member House of Representatives and a 24-member Senate, and an independent judiciary. Although the presidency was to retain executive power it was specifically forbidden to impose martial law for longer than 60 days without the approval of the legislature, which would possess the authority to revoke a martial law decree promulgated by the executive. Other provisions contained within the 18 articles of the document included the abolition of the death penalty, the prohibition of abortion, the adoption of a nuclear-free policy (subject to "national interest"), the establishment of a permanent commission to safeguard human rights and the requirement of legislative approval for any agreement concerning the leasing of Filipino territory for use by foreign powers.

There was widespread criticism of the draft document by opponents of President Aquino, particularly with regard to Concom's recommendation that she and Laurel should remain in office until 1992 when elections would be held to determine their successors. Enrile asserted that President Aquino had forfeited her mandate to govern by creating a "revolutionary government" (a reference to the abolition of the 1973 constitution under which she had been elected and its replacement by the "Freedom Constitution") and should, therefore, submit herself to fresh elections in 1987.

On February 2, 1987, the population of the Philippines voted overwhelmingly to endorse the draft constitution and thereby confirmed President Aquino in office until June 30, 1992. The final results of the plebiscite, issued by Comelec on February 7, gave a total turnout of over 87 per cent of the country's 25,000,000 registered voters, with 76.4 per cent of votes cast in favour of the draft constitution. President Aquino, who had campaigned vigorously for the endorsement of the document, welcomed the consensus amongst independent observers that the voting had been conducted fairly and that no serious irregularities had been reported and declared that the size of the turnout was proof of the population's commitment to its newly won democracy. She described her response to the result as one of "elation", and expressed the hope that the new constitution would "usher in the political stability which we all desire".

The foremost opponent of the adoption of the new constitution was Enrile, whose deteriorating relationship with the President had led to his resignation from the Cabinet in the aftermath of the attempted coup in November 1986 (see below). Whilst expressing his disappointment with the result Enrile recognized that it represented "the verdict of the people" and should, therefore, be respected. The right-wing Nationalist Party which had been the ruling party of President Marcos prior to 1978 and with which Enrile was closely associated, endorsed this position by offering the "utmost co-operation and assistance to the new government". Mr Tolentino, who had proclaimed himself acting President in an attempted coup in July 1986 accepted the legitimacy of the new constitution and accordingly dropped his claim to office.

Following the announcement of the result of the referendum a brief ceremony was held at the Malacanang Palace on February 11, and the new constitution was officially adopted in place of the "Freedom Constitution". Quoting from St Paul, "the night is over: the day is here", President Aquino led her Cabinet in swearing allegiance to the new constitution.

AQUINO'S FIRST YEAR

Threats posed by Marcos supporters and dissaffected members of the Armed Forces

There were numerous small pro-Marcos demonstrations in the first weeks of the Aquino government and, in a concerted display of force on April 13, 1986, up to 10,000 people gathered in Quezon City, the administrative capital in the north of Metro Manila, and 20,000 in Manila itself, to call for the return of the former President. After clashes with police and supporters of Aquino, some of the demonstrators began a three-week vigil outside the US embassy in protest over the US role in the ousting of Marcos. On April 27 a rally of 10,000 was addressed through an amplified telephone system by Marcos from Hawaii, where he had taken up temporary residence following his post-election flight from the Philippines. He claimed to be the "legitimate president" and urged his followers to demonstrate in his support on May 1. Many obeyed his call and violent clashes followed as his supporters fought with demonstrators loyal to Aquino. The failure of the police to contain the pro-Marcos forces led to the dismissal of district police chief, Brig.-Gen. Narcisco Cabrera.

Further fighting occurred on May 4 as police used water cannon to break up a pro-Marcos rally. On June 1 there were more clashes as supporters marching from Marcos's home province of Ilocos Norte (in the far north-west) reached the capital, where they joined a demonstration against Concom which was due to hold its inaugural meeting the following day. On June 8 gunfire, tear-gas and water cannon were used by 15,000 police to disperse demonstrators attempting to march on the presidential palace.

Although the country's senior military commanders pledged loyalty to Aquino as their President and commander-in-chief at a ceremony at Camp Aguinaldo on March 12, it was widely known that supporters of Marcos remained well represented within the armed forces. Accordingly, in an attempt to reduce the incidence of military disaffection and in line with Aquino's campaign pledges to give due consideration to the demands of the Reform the Armed Forces Movement (RAM) within the army, the new government began a far-reaching programme of military reform. Some 39 "overstaying" senior officers (who had passed the age of retirement but had retained their commissions because of their personal loyalty to Marcos) were retired in mid-March. However, a further eight generals and three colonels whose retirement was also overdue had their commands extended for six months on the recommendation of Ramos.

The reforms also included an extensive structural reorganization of the Defence Ministry initiated in late March, the widespread replacement of battalion and brigade commanders, and the breaking up of the Regional Unified Command, the highly centralized command structure of the

31

security forces created in late 1983 by Marcos and Ver. The National Intelligence Authority (which under Ver had operated as a secret police force) was dismantled, and the units which made up the 16,000-strong Presidential Security Command (which had constituted the private army of Marcos) were redeployed to other commands. The armed services were officially renamed the "New Armed Forces of the Philippines".

On May 11 the military's Anti-Graft and Corrupt Practices Board was established under the chairmanship of Brig.-Gen. Manuel Flores to examine allegations of past corruption. Investigation of prior military abuses was also begun by the Presidential Commission on Human Rights. Enrile, who advocated a general amnesty for past abuses, made clear his disapproval of the investigation on the grounds that it would damage military morale. At a rally in Cebu on May 26, Aquino announced that an amnesty would be available to some former offenders on a case-by-case basis, and pledged her willingness to "forgive" the Army's role in the assassination of her husband. She urged reconciliation between the military and the civilian population, requesting that each side "forget the past".

An unofficial inquiry began in March 1986 into the assassination of Benigno Aquino in August 1983 and into the subsequent trial and acquittal in December 1985 of 25 members of the military and one civilian. Both Mr Agapito Aquino (the brother of the dead man and head of the unofficial inquiry) and the Presidential Commission on Human Rights discovered new evidence concerning the role played by Marcos in the trial. This evidence, and a claim by the head of the original prosecution panel, Manuel Herrera, that the not guilty verdict had been predetermined, led to the establishment of a special Supreme Court commission of inquiry on June 6. The three-member commission of retired judges, which began hearing the new evidence on June 16, filed its report on July 31, 1986. The commission called upon the Supreme Court to declare a mistrial on the grounds that the original hearing had been "scripted and stage-managed" by Marcos. On September 12 the Supreme Court ordered a retrial and four days later two of the original defendants (who had continued to serve in the Army) were arrested and reportedly offered to turn state's witness. The following day warrants of arrest were issued against the remaining 24, of whom 21, comprising two generals, 18 soldiers and the sole civilian, were taken into custody. Neptali Gonzales, however, stated on September 29 that he would not seek to extradite Ver from the USA as his return to the Philippines might lead to "mischief on his part and restiveness in the military".

On July 6, 1986, meanwhile, Arturo Tolentino proclaimed himself acting President in a bid "to restore constitutional democracy to the country", and announced a Cabinet which included Enrile. Supported by 300 troops led by Brig.-Gen. Jose Maria Zumel and several thousand civilians, Tolentino commandeered a Manila hotel where he took an "oath of office" administered by a former Supreme Court justice, Serafin Cuevas. Tolentino claimed that he was taking over the presidency on the orders of Marcos, although this was later denied by the former president. Enrile immediately dissociated himself from the rebellion and surrounded the hotel and the capital's radio stations with loyal troops. Aquino, who was absent from Manila on a visit to Mindanao Island in the company of eight members of her Cabinet and Gen. Ramos, ordered that "maximum tolerance" be extended to the rebels in an effort to avoid bloodshed.

Most of the rebel troops surrendered within hours of Tolentino's proclamation, reinforcements having failed to arrive. Aquino returned to Manila as scheduled on July 7, and talks were held with the remaining rebels, who were given a 24-hour ultimatum to disperse, which they did on the morning of July 8. None of the participants was arrested and the troops and the three generals who had supported Tolentino were allowed to rejoin their units, as had been promised by Ramos. On July 9, however, Aquino announced that an independent board of inquiry would be established to investigate the extent of the Army's involvement in the incident. She demanded that Tolentino pledge his allegiance to the constitution and to her government. The passport of Tolentino and those of 24 others suspected of involvement in the rebellion were cancelled by the Ministry of Foreign Affairs, and it was suggested that charges might be brought against them. Aquino also announced the prohibition of "rallies and demonstrations designed to further the rebel cause".

Amid growing government fears concerning the loyalty of the army, on July 28 all members of the country's 250,000-strong armed forces (including the participants in the coup attempt, who had gone unpunished) were required to swear allegiance to the "Freedom Constitution". A week later the President promoted 19 senior officers to the rank of general to replace those who had been retired in March. Tolentino, who had refused to swear allegiance to the constitution and had, therefore, been charged concerning his participation in the coup attempt, agreed on August 8 to recognize the government in return for the dropping of all charges against him and other civilians implicated in the July coup attempt. On September 1 Tolentino duly took an oath in which he recognized the "existence" of the government of President Aquino and renounced the use of force as a means of effecting political change.

Enrile, who had publicly stated his "growing impatience" with the government's "leniency" in the ceasefire negotiations with the communist insurgents of the NPA, chose not to attend a Cabinet meeting on October 14, on the grounds that it was "a waste of people's money". Instead he undertook a tour of inspection of the military commands on the southern islands of Cebu and Mindanao during which he addressed several anti-communist rallies and called for a purge of those Cabinet colleagues whom he accused of having communist sympathies. Amid increasing rumours of an impending military coup, there were public calls for Enrile's resignation from several Cabinet members including the Labour and Employment Minister Augusto Sanchez (whom Mr Enrile had denounced as a communist), and the Justice Minister, Neptali Gonzales. Laurel, however, urged him to remain within the government and on October 20 cancelled a planned official visit to Indonesia in order to mediate between him and the President. A reconciliation was reported to have been effected on October 21, when President Aquino promised that her government would adopt a less conciliatory attitude towards the NPA, but on October 26 Enrile was warmly received as he addressed a crowd of 20,000 in Manila which indicated its support for Marcos and its hostility to Aquino.

On the eve of Aquino's departure for an official state visit to Japan on November 10 a large rally demonstrated its support for her as she warned "misguided elements" that any attempt at a military coup would be resisted by a mass mobilization of her supporters.

Among those participating in the rally was Rolando Olalia, the leader of the 500,000-strong *Kilusang Mayo Uno* trade union and a leading member of the recently formed left-wing People's Party (*Partido ng Bayan*). Olalia, who had earlier promised to lead a general strike in the event of a coup attempt, disappeared on November 12 after leaving a trade union meeting in Manila. The bound and mutilated corpses of Olalia and his driver were discovered the following day. In expressing her "horror and outrage" at the murders, Aquino created a committee of investigation and offered a reward of US$10,000 for information leading to the apprehension of the perpetrators. Olalia's funeral on November 20 was attended by over 100,000 mourners; meanwhile protesters staged widespread strikes and demonstrations demanding the dismissal of Enrile (who was widely believed to have been implicated in the crime), and on November 19 David Puzon, a conservative supporter of Enrile and a former member of the National Assembly, was shot dead along with two companions in an ambush in Manila.

On November 23, Aquino accepted the resignation of Enrile after allegations that he had been involved in a coup plot with elements of the Army and supporters of former President Marcos. Acting on orders issued by the President and Gen. Ramos, army units had taken up position around key sites in the capital on November 22 to prevent an attempt by officers associated with the RAM, who were loyal to Mr Enrile, to reconvene the National Assembly. In the face of the continuing loyalty of Ramos, who issued instructions to all troops to disregard orders originating either from the Defence Ministry or from those officers specifically involved in the conspiracy, the coup attempt failed to materialize.

After a Cabinet meeting on November 23, Aquino announced on television that all ministers had complied with her request to submit their resignations, and that Enrile had been succeeded as Defence Minister by Gen. Rafael Ileto, hitherto Deputy Defence Minister. She praised the "preventive measures" taken by Ramos against "the recklessness of some elements of the military", expressed regret that her "circumspection had been viewed as weakness ... and attempts at reconciliation as indecision", and stated her intention to "make a fresh start". Ileto, a retired general and former diplomat, had supported the military revolt in favour of Aquino's election victory in February 1986 and subsequently organized the President's personal bodyguard. He was reputed to be a firm opponent of communism and to command wide respect within the armed forces. Enrile officially handed over his portfolio to Ileto at a ceremony at Camp Aguinaldo on November 28, in which he claimed to be leaving office "without regret and without rancour". Ileto announced that an "informal investigation" would be held concerning the role of the military in the alleged plot.

Following Ileto's appointment, a number of other Cabinet changes were made before the remaining ministers were confirmed in their existing posts on January 3, 1987. Amongst those who lost their place in the Cabinet was Sanchez, the left-wing Labour Minister, who was replaced by his deputy Franklin Drilon, a former vice-president of the Employers' Confederation of the Philippines. The removal of Sanchez, which was widely seen as an attempt by Aquino to appease her critics on the right, led to a protest by several thousand trade unionists who picketed the Labour Ministry in Manila before being dispersed by police as they attempted to march to the presidential palace.

The position of the government was further shaken by a third attempted coup which was considerably more serious than the two which had preceded it. It began in the early hours of January 27, 1987, with co-ordinated attacks upon a total of seven military and civilian installations in Manila by army detachments totalling some 500 troops. The rebels were denied their objectives in all cases other than at the Channel 7 private broadcasting complex where a group of around 150 soldiers and 60 civilians, led by Col. Oscar Canlas, succeeded in establishing control. There followed a two-day siege of the premises as Ramos attempted to persuade the rebels to surrender without bloodshed.

One rebel soldier was reported to have been killed and several injured during the coup attempt which was believed to be linked to the planned return of Marcos. On the day before the coup it was reported that Marcos had been in telephone contact with supporters in the Philippines, and that earlier in the month his wife had purchased a consignment of combat boots and other military equipment. On January 27, Marcos spoke of his desire to return to the Philippines in order to end the country's continuing instability, and on the following day it was revealed that he had chartered a Boeing 747 airliner and was planning to fly to Manila. On January 29, however, Marcos told reporters that the US State Department had refused to allow him to leave the country and that he was being "treated like a prisoner". Canlas denied any links with Marcos and claimed that the rebellion had been prompted by the government's failure to deal effectively with the problem of communist insurgency.

In the afternoon of January 27 Aquino made a radio broadcast in which she assured the population that the coup attempt had failed and that whereas in the past such actions had been treated with tolerance, on this occasion the "full force of the law will be applied to everyone, civilian or military, who is implicated in this crime". She spoke of "the inability of some elements . . . to face the fact that civilian government is here to stay and that nothing will derail our efforts to establish full constitutional democracy". The President called upon the rebels who remained within the Channel 7 building to recognize the hopelessness of their situation and to surrender accordingly as "every moment of delay merely compounds the gravity of the crime".

The siege continued, however, and several hundred civilians gathered in the vicinity of the broadcasting station to demonstrate their support for Canlas and his men. Power and water supplies to the building were disconnected and at 10.30 p.m. on January 28, as an ultimatum for the rebels' surrender expired, tear-gas canisters were fired into the grounds of the complex. A full-scale assault on the building was prevented by the intercession of around 100 Army officers who held a five-hour meeting with Ramos during the night of January 28-29, and who persuaded him of the necessity of avoiding ordering loyal troops to fire upon their mutinous comrades.

The siege ended on the morning of January 29, after a session of talks involving Canlas, Ramos, Ileto and other senior officers. At a press conference Canlas stated that his men had not surrendered but had simply decided to obey orders to vacate the building; he also claimed that they would continue as members of the Army and that they would not be facing charges. On January 30, however, Gen. Ramos announced that 13 officers and 385 other ranks had been arrested and would face courts martial on charges ranging from mutiny to unbecoming military behaviour. Several of those charged, including Brig.-Gen. Jose Maria Zumel, the most senior of the officers, had been involved in the attempted coup of July 1986. Ramos also stated that 137 civilians had been arrested in connection with the recent coup attempt and that they would be dealt with in due course by the civilian authorities; some 100 other civilians were reported to be under investigation on suspicion of similar charges.

AQUINO'S FIRST YEAR

On February 16, the members of the 250,000-strong armed forces swore to "preserve and defend" the newly adopted constitution in a series of mass oath-taking ceremonies held at military bases throughout the country. Ileto described the document as "our supreme and fundamental law" and urged all service personnel to respect it in its entirety. Rumours of widespread disaffection within the Army continued, however, fuelled by the revelation that up to 50 per cent of army personnel had voted against adopting the new constitution in the referendum. On February 28 Ramos condemned as "divisive" the "proliferation" of "so-called fraternal organizations" within the armed forces, and demanded their dissolution.

Four people were killed and 47 injured on March 18 when a bomb exploded at the Philippine Military Academy in Baguio city (120 miles north of Manila) during a rehearsal for a graduation ceremony. It was widely believed that the intended target of the bomb had been President Aquino herself, who was due to preside over the annual passing-out ceremony for military cadets on March 22.

Although she admitted that she had been "profoundly shaken" by the news of the incident, the President visited those wounded in the attack and then attended the ceremony as planned. In her speech to the cadets she described it as "ironic" that the greatest threat to her life since taking office should have occurred in a military establishment, and she promised to track down the perpetrators of "this most treacherous . . . and dastardly act of cowardice". She stated that her "offers of peace and reconciliation" had been met with "the most bloody and insolent rejections by the left and the right" and that her future policy would concentrate not on "social and economic reform but police and military action".

Initial reports had suggested that the attack had been conducted by the NPA, although the organization immediately denied any involvement. Forensic examination of the bomb's construction and design later indicated that it had originated from within the armed forces, and on March 23 an officer, three enlisted men and six civilians were detained in connection with the bombing. The officer, Capt. Wilhelm Doromal, was an instructor at the Academy in the use of explosives and a senior member of a right-wing Army faction known as the "Guardian Brotherhood", members of which were believed to have been involved in the attempted coup in January. The Guardians were later implicated in other plans to overthrow the government.

Fighting broke out at Fort Bonifacio on April 18 when an attempt was made to free over 100 men who were being held in connection with the January coup attempt. A dozen soldiers, led by a former sergeant of the defunct Presidential Security Command, Ernest Librado, forced their way into the base shortly before dawn. The assailants surrendered after several hours of fighting during which about 40 of the prisoners and nine of the guards joined in on the side of the rebels; one was killed, several were injured and 19 of the prisoners escaped.

Earlier, on April 13, it was reported that a plan had been uncovered in which rebel soldiers were intending to take over the International School in Manila, hold American and other pupils hostage, seize radio and television stations and force the government and Gen. Ramos to resign. The attempt was frustrated when the plot was discovered and troops were confined to barracks. The soldiers involved, estimated to number between 100 and 300, were members of a hitherto unknown military fraternity called *Tiwark* ("Upside Down"), and were thought to include members of the Presidential Security Command, many of whom had deserted after the flight of Marcos.

Negotiations with communist insurgents

On June 5, 1986, Aquino announced an agreement to begin formal negotiations with the Communist Party of the Philippines (CPP). The talks would aim to establish a ceasefire in the 17-year insurgency campaign conducted by the CPP's military wing, the New People's Army (NPA). The emissaries appointed to represent the NPA were a senior member of the CPP central committee, Satur Ocampo (a former journalist who had escaped from government detention in 1985 after serving nine years), and Antonio Zumel, the chairman of the National Democratic Front (NDF). On June 26 Aquino named the Agriculture Minister, Ramon Mitra, and the Presidential Human Rights Commission chairman, Jose Diokno, as the government representatives for the talks. The location, agenda, and starting date of the talks were not disclosed, but on July 2 Mitra said that an initial meeting between the two sides had taken place.

After her election, Aquino had honoured her campaign pledge by calling for a ceasefire and offered an amnesty to those guerrillas who were prepared to lay down their arms. On March 14, however, the CPP central committee suggested that it was unrealistic to expect guerrillas to surrender their weapons before an end to the fighting had been negotiated. It also claimed that no meaningful negotiations could begin whilst the personnel and apparatus of the former regime remained in place. Nevertheless, on March 24 the NPA and NDF issued separate statements recognizing the reforms of the Aquino regime and agreeing to consider undertaking ceasefire talks without preconditions.

It had been suggested that splits had developed within the NPA concerning its response to the new government. On April 29 Fr Conrado Balweg, a senior guerrilla commander in the Cordillera mountain region (the central northern part of Luzon Island), announced that he and his troops had left the NPA to establish the Cordillera People's Liberation Army (CPLA), and that he was planning to begin peace negotiations with the authorities. It was also reported that an increasing number of guerrillas had accepted appeals from the Church and the government to surrender their arms.

Fighting continued, however, between government forces and other units of the NPA, which were estimated to be up to 30,000 strong and in effective control of 20 per cent of rural Filipino territory. On June 4 Ramos announced that 375 NPA guerrillas had been killed in clashes with the security forces since the election of Aquino. In addition 46 members of the Mindanao-based Moslem secessionist movement Moro National Liberation Front (MNLF) had been killed and a total of 358 government forces and 261 civilians had died.

Negotiations officially began between representatives of the government and emissaries from the NDF in Manila on August 5, but were impeded initially by procedural wrangles and a dispute over the duration of safe-conduct passes issued by the military to the NDF negotiators. Twelve soldiers were killed on August 25 when an army patrol was ambushed in the Zamboanga del Sur province (Mindanao) as sporadic fighting continued throughout the Philippines.

On September 13 President Aquino signed a separate peace pact with Fr Balweg and, following further negotiations, an agreement was signed on December 15, whereby the CPLA became a participant in the newly created Cordillera Regional Development Council, which had been established to consider the formation of a Cordillera autonomous region. The CPLA also began to receive military assistance from the government. During 1987 an interim administration was created in the Cordillera (prior to the negotiation of full autonomy) within which the CPLA was a participant. In practice, however, the CPLA appeared to enjoy little support in the region itself, while the Regional Development Council excluded the Cordillera People's Alliance, an umbrella organization of some 120 tribal and local organizations.

By the end of September, it was widely reported that a ceasefire was shortly to be signed by the NDF based upon negotiations which had followed a government offer of a 30-day truce made on September 6. The talks were suspended by the NDF representatives, however, after the arrest on September 30 of Rodolfo Salas, a leading member of the outlawed CPP. The arrest was made outside a Manila hospital where Salas was seeking medical attention in the company of his wife and his bodyguard. The NDF condemned the arrest as a breach of faith on the part of the authorities; Salas did not actually possess a safe-conduct pass, but the NDF claimed that as a party to the negotiations he had had *de facto* immunity from arrest. The NDF also regarded the arrest of Salas as an attempt by the military to prevent the signing of a ceasefire (Enrile having consistently maintained that a ceasefire would enable the NPA to regroup its forces and thus prosecute its insurgency campaign with greater effect).

Salas was charged with rebellion on October 2, but his companions, although charged with lesser crimes, were released from detention on October 14 in an effort to restart the ceasefire negotiations. Two days later Aquino travelled to the island of Panay for talks with regional NPA leaders. The Manila negotiations were resumed on October 18, but little progress was made and on October 28 the President threatened to initiate a major new military offensive unless there was a breakthrough in the talks before the end of November.

The offer of a 100-day truce was made by the NDF on November 1 and, although openly criticized by Enrile as being too advantageous to the guerrillas, it provided the basis for further negotiation. An agreement was eventually reached on outstanding issues and was due to be signed on November 14 but the talks were again suspended by the NDF following the murder of Olalia. They were resumed on November 25 (after the resignation of Enrile and the arrest of an army sergeant and a civilian in connection with Olalia's death) and a 60-day truce was signed on November 27. The agreement, which became operational on December 10, outlawed "hostile acts" by either side. It provided for the establishment of a National Ceasefire Committee, assisted by local committees, to supervise the truce, and stipulated that further talks should be held in January 1987 aimed at settling "substantive issues" and producing a permanent peace settlement. The right of the NPA to collect taxes in those areas under its control was not recognized although nor was such activity defined as a breach of the terms of the truce. The guerrillas promised not to carry arms in the vicinity of population centres and it was pledged that the Army would suspend its military operations and inform local ceasefire committees before entering areas of known guerrilla activity.

Although the terms of the ceasefire were generally respected the two sides failed to make progress when negotiations were resumed in early January 1987. On January 2 the government announced its rejection of demands by the NDF to include on the agenda the issues of foreign debt repudiation, the release of Salas, the future of the US military bases, the nationalization of industry or the incorporation of NDF or NPA elements in the government or the armed forces. At the first session of talks on January 6, the two sides merely agreed to a joint general commitment to "food and freedom, jobs and justice", and arranged to meet again on January 13. In separate statements to the press both Ramos and Antonio Zumel, the chief NDF negotiator, suggested that an extension of the ceasefire beyond its 60-day limit (i.e. beyond February 8) was unlikely unless the two sides could achieve a significant breakthrough.

The 100-day truce expired on February 8, 1987, following the failure of negotiations to make any further progress towards agreeing upon the basis of a more permanent settlement. The talks were officially broken off on January 30, although the terms of the ceasefire were respected until February 8, when fighting was resumed with over 50 people being reported killed within the first three days. Amongst these were 17 inhabitants of the village of Namulandayan, 60 miles north of Manila in Nueva Ecija province, who were killed by troops after an army patrol clashed with NPA forces sheltering within the settlement. Initially it had been suggested that the dead had been NPA guerrillas, but a commission of inquiry established to examine the incident found them to have been civilians, and suggested that they had been murdered by the troops in retaliation for the villagers' provision of aid to the NPA. Six officers and 79 soldiers alleged to have been involved in the incident were later placed under restriction by Ramos pending further investigation.

Peace negotiations with Moslem secessionists

A delegation from the MNLF arrived in Manila on March 8, 1986, and began talks on March 13 aimed at the negotiation of a peaceful conclusion to the 16-year war of secession. The delegation represented two factions within the MNLF: the Moslem Islamic Liberation Front (MILF) led by the head of the MNLF political committee Hashim Salamat, based mainly in Lanao del Sur and reportedly supported by Egypt, and the smaller Bangsa Moro National Liberation Front (BMNLF) led by Dimas Pundato and reportedly backed by Saudi Arabia. Although no representative from the largest and most militant MNLF faction was present, it was suggested that its leader, Nur Misuari, the MNLF central committee president, who was linked with Libya and in recent years increasingly with Iran, might join the talks at a later stage if they were seen to be making progress.

The MILF and the BMNLF had suggested a willingness to compromise over the issue of complete independence for the predominantly Moslem areas of Mindanao and the neighbouring islands of the Sulu Sea. Both factions called for the complete implementation of the Tripoli agreement signed with the Marcos government in 1976 which had provided for regional autonomy for the nation's 13 southern provinces. During her election campaign Mrs Aquino had pledged "to respect and substantiate" Moslem aspirations for autonomy.

Despite pleas for patience from Agapito Aquino, who had been largely responsible for the negotiations on the government's behalf, the Moslem delegation left Manila on April 25 after claiming that the government was not committed to the talks. Negotiations were resumed on September 5, however, when President Aquino flew to the southern island of Jolo for talks with Nur Misuari. Following the talks the participants suggested that they were "optimistic" about the chances of negotiating a long-term peace settlement to end the Moslem secessionist struggle, and announced that they had agreed to maintain the tentative ceasefire (in force since late August) and to undertake substantive negotiations under the auspices of the Islamic Conference Organization (ICO) before the end of the year.

At the invitation of President Aquino, Misuari had returned to the Philippines, after 10 years of self-imposed exile in the Middle East, following several sessions of talks with Agapito Aquino. He attended an MNLF congress in Jolo on September 3-5, and was reported to have spoken in favour of a negotiated peace settlement on the basis of legislative and judicial autonomy for predominantly Moslem areas, rather than continuing the conflict in an effort to secure complete Moslem independence, which President Aquino had repeatedly stressed was unacceptable.

The MILF and the BMNLF were reported to have expressed their support for the agreement, having suggested in earlier talks with the government their willingness to settle for autonomy as opposed to complete independence. Sporadic violence continued, however; in one widely reported incident on September 7 an unidentified paramilitary group attacked the congregation of a Roman Catholic church in Salvador, killing 10 people and wounding more than 90.

Following three days of talks with Agapito Aquino in Jeddah, Saudi Arabia, Misuari announced on January 4, 1987, that he had signed an agreement modifying his original demand for Moslem independence in favour of accepting "full autonomy". Further talks were scheduled to take place after the constitutional referendum to define the term "full autonomy" and Misuari added that he was negotiating with representatives of Salamat in an effort to establish a common position in advance of these.

On January 13, however, the MILF launched a campaign of co-ordinated attacks on bridges, power supplies and government buildings in western Mindanao, and fierce fighting was reported to have occurred between MILF units and those of the MNLF and the Army, resulting in the deaths of at least 30 people. A truce was negotiated on January 17, only 24 hours before President Aquino was due to arrive in the area as part of her constitutional ratification campaign. She held talks with representatives of the MILF in Cotabato City and was reported to have renewed her invitation to Mr Salamat to participate fully in the forthcoming autonomy talks scheduled to be held in Manila on February 9. Although members of the MNLF and the BMNLF were represented at the meeting, those from the MILF failed to attend. A further session of talks was held in Zamboanga City on February 20 (although once again the MILF chose not to participate), at which the MNLF delegation presented its proposals for "full autonomy" which were believed to include the establishment of an autonomous regional legislature, judiciary and armed forces.

The Mendiola bridge massacre

In one of the most publicly damaging incidents since President Aquino came to power, over 20 people were killed in central Manila on January 22, 1987, when troops opened fire upon a demonstration composed largely of peasants demanding government action on land reform. The 10,000 demonstrators had intended to march to the Malacanang Palace to address their grievances to the President, but were halted at the nearby Mendiola Bridge by troops and police. The shooting followed the throwing of stones and bottles by some of the demonstrators, but it appeared that no warning shots were fired and medical evidence later suggested that several of the dead had been shot in the back whilst attempting to flee. After an emergency Cabinet meeting President Aquino appeared on national television shortly before midnight to express her shock and sadness over the incident and to promise that "the persons responsible for this tragedy, whichever side they belong to, will be held to the fullest account". Ramos issued a statement on January 23, in which he admitted that troops involved in the incident had over-reacted and that he had ordered a complete review of crowd control procedures. The officer responsible for the order to open fire, Brig.-Gen. Ramon Montamo, was placed on indefinite leave pending the results of a presidential commission of inquiry.

The killings were widely and vehemently condemned by those of all political persuasions including staunch supporters of President Aquino such as Cardinal Sin, who suggested that the government's failure to deal adequately with the issue of land reform had caused the tragedy. The government's culpability with regard to the massacre was also cited in the resignations of five of the seven members of the Presidential Commission on Human Rights.

On January 26, a demonstration of over 20,000 marched to the site of the killing and, despite the misgivings of the police, was allowed to cross the Mendiola Bridge and approach the gates of the Malacanang Palace. The marchers were met by Aquino and members of her Cabinet who linked arms with them in a symbolic act of reconciliation and as an assurance that they would not be molested by police or troops. Before moving on and dispersing peacefully, representations were delivered to members of the government calling for an acceleration of the land reform programme.

In its report of February 27, the commission of inquiry criticized the use of "raw marine recruits" to police the demonstration and recommended that those soldiers and police who had been photographed shooting into the crowd should be prosecuted. It also recommended the prosecution of the peasant activist Jaime Tadeo, who had led the march and, it was claimed, had exhorted the demonstrators to attempt to cross the bridge in defiance of the security forces. A presidential spokesman welcomed the findings as "even handed" and stated that the report would be forwarded to the the Ministry of Justice for "appropriate action".

Despite the mounting problems facing the regime, the first anniversary of Marcos's fall was widely celebrated in rallies and religious services in Manila and elsewhere on February 25, which had earlier been declared a national holiday. President Aquino gave an address to troops at Camp Aguinaldo (which had been opened to the public for the occasion), in which she praised the role of the military in liberating the population from the tyranny of the Marcos regime by choosing to "disobey the dictator in obedience to the higher call of freedom". She then attended an open-air mass conducted by Cardinal Sin and later urged the assembled crowds to preserve "the selflessness and dedication" embodied within the "People Power" phenomenon.

THE CONGRESSIONAL ELECTIONS

Three months after the formal adoption of the constitution, the Aquino regime faced its next test with the congressional elections of May 11, 1987. Under the terms of the new constitution, the 24 members of the Senate (the upper chamber of the bicameral legislature) were elected by a list system from amongst native Filipino citizens of at least 35 years of age, and could sit for no more than two consecutive six-year terms. Members of the House of Representatives, who were eligible for no more than three consecutive three-year terms in office, consisted of 200 elected members and up to 50 members appointed by the President to represent minority interests. A total of 89 candidates contested the Senate elections, while 1,899 stood for the House of Representatives.

Support for the government was again grouped in the People's Struggle—Laban (*Lakas ng Bayan*) and the United Nationalist Democratic Organization (Unido).

The major opposition grouping was the Grand Alliance for Democracy (GAD), a coalition of disparate (though largely conservative) elements which included former supporters and opponents of Mr Marcos, and which was led by Juan Ponce Enrile and Arturo Tolentino. Candidates were also announced by numerous smaller parties including those members of the *Kilusang Bagong Lipunan* (Marcos's New Society Movement) who remained outside the GAD. The *Partido ng Bayan* (People's Party—PNB) a left-wing group established in 1986 by Jose Maria Sison of the banned Communist Party of the Philippines, was initially prohibited by Comelec, the election commission, from participating in the elections because of its commitment to the concept of "class war". This decision was later rescinded following changes in the stated aims of the PNB, although during the campaign there were instances of police raids upon party premises and arrests of suspected members of the New People's Army. Among the PNB's candidates for election to the Senate was Bernabe Buscayno, the alleged founder of the NPA.

In many areas of the country the campaign was highly confused, with numerous candidates for the House of Representatives claiming to have been endorsed by President Aquino, and frequently facing opposition from fellow members of their own party (this problem apparently

45

applying to Laban and Unido as well as to those parties which opposed the government). Although there were allegations of isolated instances of vote-buying and intimidation of voters, the campaign was generally perceived to have been fairer than any which had been held under the Marcos regime, and to have been free of any systematic attempt to interfere with the legitimate procedure of the poll. The official number of deaths resulting from election-related violence was calculated at 63 (compared with 158 deaths during the 1986 presidential campaign), with up to half of the victims thought to be campaign workers for the PNB.

The Roman Catholic Church maintained a low profile throughout the campaign in accordance with instructions issued by Cardinal Sin. During the course of the campaign, however, Cardinal Sin issued a pastoral letter in which he endorsed a number of President Aquino's senatorial candidates and condemned those on the right and left of the political spectrum who were prepared to sanction violence as a mechanism of social and political change.

Within hours of the polls closing on the evening of May 11, it became clear that the government of President Aquino had won an impressive victory. On May 13, Enrile and other leading members of the GAD addressed a rally of 3,000 supporters during which they accused the administration of having engaged in electoral fraud on a massive scale thereby distorting the democratic wishes of the population and rendering the election results invalid. "We know we have won the election. . . . We were cheated", Mr Enrile stated, and he warned: "We will do what we can to achieve justice in our country." The chairman of Comelec, Ramon Felipe, dismissed Enrile's complaints and insisted that the voting (which he estimated to have involved over 90 per cent of the electorate) was largely fair. This view was supported both by President Aquino and by the National Citizens' Movement for Free Elections (Namfrel), the unofficial citizens' electoral monitoring group. On May 27, the Supreme Court dismissed an application by the GAD to halt the count and ruled that there was no evidence of irregularities on a scale sufficient to invalidate the result.

When the results of the Senate elections were declared by Comelec in early June, it emerged that candidates aligned with Aquino had won 22 seats and the GAD the remaining two (Enrile and Joseph Estrada, a film star and former Mayor of San Juan district in Manila).

Enrile's candidacy for the Senate had been challenged by Augusto Sanchez, the former leftist Minister of Labour, who finished in 25th place in the Senate elections, with only 72,000 votes fewer than Enrile. Sanchez complained that although Comelec had disqualified a nuisance candidate with the same name as himself at the outset of the campaign, the bogus candidate's name had inadvertently been left on voting lists, thereby depriving the former minister of a significant number of votes in several areas of the country. Comelec admitted the error and delayed the confirmation of Enrile's election until the matter had been fully investigated and a recount conducted. Enrile was eventually proclaimed as the 24th Senator on August 13 on orders of the Supreme Court, despite widespread scepticism as to the validity of the result.

Counting for the House of Representatives continued into July, and, by the time of the official opening of Congress on July 27, 13 seats remained in dispute. At this stage, Aquino's supporters held 127 seats, and of the remainder, 25 had been won by independents (some of whom claimed presidential endorsement), 33 by the right-wing opposition (including nine KBL members) and two by the PNB.

The results were dismissed as fraudulent by several senior members of the NPA, who alleged numerous instances of officially sanctioned intimidation against representatives of the PNB, and claimed that the election had been reduced to "a mere contest of personalities, patronage and machinery, both bureaucratic and military". They warned that the NPA would respond by stepping up its armed struggle in an effort to counter the "illusion about the Aquino government of earnestness and sincerity in carrying out reforms".

Prior to the inauguration of the Congress, when legislative authority would be formally transferred from the executive to the newly elected legislature, Aquino took the opportunity to enact a series of presidential decrees on a wide range of issues.

These included provision for local elections in November 1987, an increase in the maximum penalty for association with the NPA or other anti-government rebels from 12 years' to life imprisonment, and the sanctioning of a "citizens' army" to assist the security forces in their fight against the guerrilla insurgents. This proposed 1,000,000-strong force was designed to replace the paramilitary Civilian Home Defence Force of 65,000, which was widely perceived as corrupt, inefficent and having engaged in widespread human rights abuses. Several decrees enacted by former President Marcos were repealed, including that which prescribed the death penalty for assassination attempts upon the President or members of the President's family.

Before surrendering jurisdiction over military appointments to the Senate, the President announced on June 27 that the Deputy Chief of Staff, Maj.-Gen. Salvador Misson, and the Army Commander, Maj.-Gen. Rodolfo Canieso, would retire at the end of the month and would be replaced respectively by Maj.-Gen. Renato de Villa and Brig.-Gen. Restituto Padilla.

REVOLUTION IN THE PHILIPPINES?

Presidential address to Congress

In her inaugural address to both Houses on July 27, President Aquino welcomed the revival of Filipino democracy but warned that the country continued to face the threat of "totalitarian slavery on the left and reversion to fascist terror and corruption on the right". Contrary to expectation she failed to outline the proposed legislative programme of her government, choosing instead to concentrate upon a vehement denunciation of foreign creditors whom she castigated for their reluctance to offer concessions on servicing the country's US$28,000 million debt (much of which had been incurred by the Marcos regime). Her speech drew enthusiastic applause from the assembled congressmen, although many commentators saw it as a tactic to avoid publicly committing her administration to potentially unpopular policies.

Local elections

Elections to more than 16,000 local government offices took place on January 18, 1988. Although voting was generally peaceful, a total of 103 people, including 39 candidates, died in election-related violence in the weeks leading up to the vote and on polling day itself. Preliminary results suggested that a number of close associates of President Aquino had failed to gain office, and some observers saw the elections as representing something of a return to the "guns and goons" style of Filipino politics, with powerful local figures ensuring electoral success by a mixture of patronage and coercion. In areas controlled by the NPA, candidates paid the guerrillas for "permits to campaign", thereby making a substantial contribution to the NPA's funds.

A number of controversial candidates gained office in the elections; among these were Lt.-Col. Rofoldo Aguinaldo (one of the leaders of the August 1987 coup attempt — see below), who was elected Governor of Cagayan Province, and Col. Rolando Abadilla, currently in detention following his arrest in July 1987 in connection with earlier coup plots, as Vice-Governor of Ilocos Norte (ex-President Marcos's home province). Abadilla was sworn in at a ceremony at the base where he was being held, prior to being returned to detention.

PART TWO

THE THREAT FROM THE RIGHT

Although the approval of the constitution and the successes of the administration's supporters in the congressional elections seemed to clear the way for a period of democratic stability in the Philippines, the regime continued to face violent threats from the right-wing opposition, sections of which saw their failure in the polls as the cue for attempts to overthrow the government by force.

To some extent, the right was divided between those who maintained links with ex-President Marcos and actively worked for his return, and those whose main concern was with what they saw as the new regime's failure to give adequate support to the armed forces and to prosecute the war against the guerrillas with sufficient vigour. On the whole, the most serious threat was posed by the second group, who enjoyed widespread support within the armed forces, including officers who had helped to overthrow Marcos and who had no wish to see his return. For many of them, former Defence Minister Juan Ponce Enrile was the preferred leader, although after his dismissal from the Cabinet at the end of 1986, he refrained from giving public support to any military attack on the government. The distinction between the two groups was not clear-cut, however, and there was concern across the the whole of the right wing at the presence of alleged leftists and communist sympathizers in the Aquino government.

Revelations of pro-Marcos coup plots

The US administration announced on July 8, 1987, that Marcos and his wife, Imelda, had been banned from leaving the island of Hawaii (where they had lived since the February 1986 revolution) after it had learned via tape-recorded conversations that they planned to return to the Philippines on July 10 as part of an armed uprising against Aquino. The tapes, which had been secretly recorded on May 21 by Robert Hirschfeld, a lawyer, and an associate posing as an arms dealer, were played to a US congressional sub-committee on Asia and the Pacific on July 9.

On the tapes, Marcos claimed that he had a force of 10,000 people in the Philippines ready to stage the uprising, which would involve taking President Cory Aquino as a hostage. He listed a number of arms requirements, including tanks, Stinger anti-aircraft missiles, and a variety of small arms. He claimed to have between US$500,000,000 ans $1,000 million available in Swiss bank accounts and also referred to a cache of 1,000 tonnes of gold (worth approximately $14,000 million), the whereabouts of which were known only to himself. This so-called "Marcos gold" was believed to consist of treasure from various Asian countries plundered by Japanese forces during the Second World War and buried by Gen. Tomoyuki Yamashita, the Japanese military commander in the Philippines, as his forces retreated from the country at the end of the war. The existence of the gold itself was in doubt, and it was thought highly unlikely that Marcos would know where it was.

The retired US General, John Singlaub, had led a US team to the Philippines in February, supposedly to search for the treasure. Reports at the time suggested that Singlaub, currently chairman of the World Anti-Communist League and an old friend of Marcos, had in fact been training army units and vigilantes in techniques of "low-intensity conflict" in areas where communist guerrillas were active.

In another incident, an army major arrested on July 13 gave details of a right-wing pro-Marcos plot to seize air force headquarters at Villamor and the adjacent international airport and launch a coup against the government from there. Others arrested over the ensuing days included Col. Rolando Abadilla, the former head of the military intelligence bureau under Marcos, who was suspected of having played a central role in the mutinies of January and April. As head of the intelligence bureau, Abadilla was reported to have organized the torture and murder of political prisoners.

A number of small bombs which exploded in Manila during late July were described by a military spokesman as part of an attempt to interfere with the opening of Congress on July 27. The bombs had been placed in the US embassy library, a church and business premises, as well as in Cardinal Jaime Sin's residence. They contained little explosive, however, and caused only four minor casualties.

In an effort to combat the growing level of armed lawlessness, the government announced a series of new security measures on August 12. Special courts would be set up to try offences connected with such matters as sedition, subversion, the illegal possession of firearms and drug trafficking. The courts would be empowered to impose sentences of life imprisonment. In addition, the number of military checkpoints would be increased as part of a drive against unauthorized private armies and other armed groups. By the end of the year, it was clear that little if any progress had been made in this field.

REVOLUTION IN THE PHILIPPINES?

The lead-up to the August coup attempt

The most serious threat yet posed to the Aquino regime took the form of a major coup attempt by disaffected sections of the Army on August 27-28. The attempt followed a fortnight of demonstrations and strikes organized by left-wing organizations and trade unions protesting against government economic policy.

A wave of protests was triggered by the announcement on August 14 of an 18 per cent increase in fuel prices. A series of demonstrations were held in Manila on August 21 (anniversary of the 1983 assassination of President Aquino's husband, Benigno), during which marchers chanted "Down with Cory!" and demanded the immediate reversal of the increases. The United Association of Transport Workers (UATW), involving mainly bus company employees together with jeepney drivers, staged a one-day strike in Manila and elsewhere on August 24. The following day Aquino announced a partial reversal of the increases. This failed to meet the protestors' demands, however, and on August 26 workers in a large number of sectors responded to a general strike call by the Kilusang Mayo Uno (KMU) trade union federation, which affected about half the country. During the day, demonstrators clashed with police, particularly in Manila and Cebu, and there were numerous injuries and arrests as police broke up protest gatherings with water cannon and truncheons. Reports that police had opened fire on demonstrators in Bacoor (on the southern outskirts of Manila) were denied by official spokesmen.

The day after the strike, police arrested 71 people, mostly labour leaders, on charges of "incitement to sedition"; those held included Medardo Roda, the UATW chairman. Other labour leaders went into hiding, including the KMU chairman, Crispin Beltran. The Manila police chief, Brig.-Gen. Alfredo Lim, said that he had personally ordered the arrests. The presidential spokesman, Teodoro Benigno, said that Aquino herself had no specific comment to make on the arrests, but added that the police had been ordered to arrest demonstrators who resorted to "illegal measures" such as the erection of barricades.

The August coup attempt: rebel attacks on the presidential palace and the army headquarters

The coup attempt started in the late evening of August 27, when about 300 rebel soldiers entered Manila, attacked the Malacanang palace and seized two television stations, Channels 9 and 13. (A third station was seized in the early hours of August 28.) Rebel units also surrounded the National Assembly building and occupied the Camelot Hotel. Loyalist troops surrounded the palace and overcame the rebels by about 3 a.m. on August 28. Benigno Aquino (Cory's son), was wounded during the early stages of the fighting, in which three of his bodyguards were killed.

Gen. Ramos, the Armed Forces Chief of Staff, did not declare his loyalty to the regime until 3 a.m., leading to speculation that he had waited until it was clear that the immediate threat to the regime had passed.

The US Administration repeatedly stated its strong support for Aquino throughout the day. Aquino herself made repeated television and radio broadcasts during August 28, in which she assured the public that the coup attempt had been crushed (despite evidence to the contrary during the first half of the day). She described the rebels as traitors who should be shot on sight.

Early on August 28, rebel troops captured Camp Aguinaldo, the army headquarters in northern Manila, forcing Ramos and other senior officers to flee. Some of the Camp was destroyed in the fighting. Air Force headquarters at Villamor was also the scene of heavy fighting, where the rebels were commanded by Col. Tito Legaspi, a close associate of Enrile. Rebel activity was also reported in other areas, notably Cebu, where Brig. Eduardo Abenida, accusing the government of being "soft on communists" led a force which took over provincial administrative offices, banks and broadcasting stations. (These were later handed back to civilian control.)

The overall leader of the coup was Col. Gregorio "Gringo" Honasan, aged 39, a popular figure associated with right-wing circles who had a nationwide reputation for his leading role in the military opposition to the Marcos regime in the period leading to its overthrow. He had a distinguished academic and military record, and had been commended for bravery in the fight against the Moslem separatists in Mindanao. Following Marcos's departure, Honasan became Enrile's security chief, and, after the latter's dismissal from the Cabinet in November 1986, Honasan was posted to Fort Magasaysay, 100 miles east of Manila, from where he launched the coup attempt. His name had also been linked to earlier efforts to overthrow Aquino.

In broadcasts over armed forces radio and in telephone calls to press agencies during the coup attempt, Honasan and his associates claimed that their action was based on dissatisfaction with the government's attitude towards the NPA and its handling of the insurgency. They repeatedly denied any loyalty to Marcos. Speaking from Hawaii, Marcos himself insisted that he had no involvement with the rebels, and had had no prior knowledge of the coup, adding that "I promised the American government that I would not have anything to do with destabilization (of the Aquino government), and I intend to fulfil that promise". He did state, however, that he would be ready to return to the Philippines if asked, although he expected that "they might choose someone else".

Both Enrile and the other opposition Senator, Joseph Estrada, went to ground during the fighting. They failed to attend an emergency session of both houses of Congress, held on the afternoon of Aug. 28, which pledged loyalty to Aquino and the constitution (although a number of Senators urged careful consideration of the Army's grievances and called for an inquiry into military morale, pay and equipment). In a speech on August 31, Enrile termed the revolt "idealistic", claiming that it was "only a symptom of our national condition" and of the government's "fundamental inability" to bring about decisive changes in national affairs. He accused the government of being responsible for the "political instability" dominating the country.

On September 4, police in Manila seized a cache of weapons and army uniforms in a building occupied by one of Enrile's business enterprises.

The recapture of Camp Aguinaldo and the defeat of the rebels

The loyalist counter-attack was delayed by a shortage of men and equipment, as well as poor telephone communications and frequent vehicle breakdowns. Early on August 28, however, they succeeded in dislodging rebels from their positions around the National Assembly and the Camelot Hotel, although about 100 rebels remained entrenched inside the building.

The first attacks on Camp Aguinaldo, at about 11 a.m., were beaten off by rebel sniper fire. These and subsequent operations were hampered by the crowds of civilians who gathered to watch the battles and cheer on the loyalist troops. In their eagerness to get a close view of the fighting, many were caught in the crossfire, and there was a large number of civilian casualties. It was also reported that soldiers on both sides in the Aguinaldo battles deliberately shot wide in an attempt to avoid killing each other. The attitude of the loyalist troops apparently hardened, however, after one of their number had been killed by a sniper, and as the day wore on, Manila experienced its heaviest fighting since the Second World War. The Camp was bombed by aircraft twice during the afternoon, and loyalist troops eventually gained entry via armoured cars in the early evening. Rebel resistance was not finally overcome until after nightfall, by which time Honasan and several of his close associates had escaped by helicopter. The soldiers holding out in the Camelot Hotel surrendered at about the same time after being strafed by helicopter gunships.

THE THREAT FROM THE RIGHT

In a broadcast on September 2, President Aquino claimed that a total of 1,350 soldiers had taken part in the rebellion, including 50 officers. She gave the casualty toll as 53 killed (19 rebels, 12 loyalists and 22 civilians, including a New Zealand journalist) and 100 soldiers injured (61 loyalists and 39 rebels). The total number of civilians injured was never ascertained. In the same broadcast, Aquino claimed that the government had known of the coup plans two weeks in advance. She failed to explain, however, why this knowledge had not enabled them to be better prepared for the attacks.

At a press conference on September 1, Gen. Ramos, who had himself been strongly criticized by the rebels, admitted that the rebellion had seriously weakened the Army's ability to fight the NPA and Moslem separatists. He promised that the ringleaders of the coup would be dealt with severely, but that those who had merely followed instructions would be more leniently treated.

On September 7, some 800 captured rebels who had been held in two tank landing ships in Manila Bay were brought ashore and reassigned to their units for normal duties. Seventeen army officers, including Honasan and three generals, were dismissed from the armed forces, and, together with 21 others, charged on September 28 with the specimen offence of murder of a police sergeant during fighting for control of the Channel 4 television station.

In the week following the coup, there were widespread allegations in the press and Congress that US officials had been seen with rebel forces, giving rise to accusations that the USA was pursuing a "twin-track" policy of backing both the Aquino government and those attempting to overthrow it. Statements by Philippines army officers subsequently confirmed that a US military attaché, Lt.-Col. Victor Raphael, had visited rebel positions at Villamor air base during the early hours of the rebellion. Raphael was reportedly a close friend of Honasan. US officials confirmed Raphael's presence at the base, but added that he had warned the rebels that US aid would be severed if the coup succeeded. However, other reports from Philippines army sources said that he had attempted to persuade loyalist troops to join the rebellion. Against a background of mounting demand from Philippines congressmen for a full inquiry into the allegations, Raphael was on October 28 recalled to Washington. The move was thought to be a result of strong pressure from the newly appointed Foreign Secretary, Raul Manglapus. On November 10, the Philippines House of Representatives authorized a special investigation into allegations that three US military attachés had been involved in the coup attempt.

Rebel activity continued in the provinces around the capital and in Cebu for several days after the crushing of the mutiny in Manila itself. The movement also enjoyed strong support among junior officers and soldiers in north-eastern areas of Luzon, notably Cagayan, where Lt.-Col. Rodolfo Aguinaldo, one of the Army's leading counter-insurgency fighters who had been relieved of his post as Cagayan's military commander after the mutiny, was still calling publicly for Aquino's overthrow two weeks later. There was some evidence that he was trying, in conjunction with Honasan, to establish a new base for rebel action in the area.

A document put out on August 31 in Baguio (where the élite Philippines Military Academy was based) declared the establishment of a "ruling junta" and a provisional government. The document, which was unsigned but believed to emanate from Honasan, accused the government of treason and softness in its approach towards the NPA and the Moslem insurgents and called for fresh presidential elections. Since it declared that the country had been placed under the control of the provisional government until conditions had been stabilized, it was assumed that it had been originally intended for publication in the event of the coup attempt succeeding.

Honasan himself remained at large for three months, making periodic anti-Aquino statements via the press and radio in which he appealed to people to support him to prevent a drift back to the old abuses of the Marcos era. In an effort to exert some sort of control over the media, the government on October 7 ordered the closure of three radio stations on the grounds that they had broadcast rebel propaganda. Honasan was eventually captured on December 9 in a Manila suburb in a house owned by Guillermo Fernandez, formerly Enrile's private secretary. Honasan had been about to give an interview to an American journalist when 50 soldiers broke into the house, capturing him and four other officers together with a civilian. One of the other leading figures in the coup attempt, Lt.-Col. Robert Navida, surrendered on November 17 to the Air Force Chief of Staff, Gen. Antonio Soleto, whom he had tried to capture during the coup.

In the months following the August coup attempt, rumours of imminent further action by rebel troops flew back and forth, and the atmosphere in the capital remained tense. Troops and tanks were deployed around Manila on September 30 after it had been reported that 1,000 disloyal troops might be planning another action. Most were withdrawn by the evening and an army spokesman said that rumours of unauthorized troop movements were completely untrue; the Army nevertheless remained on alert. Other factors contributed to the tension, including a power cut in Camp Aguinaldo which was seen as a prelude to rebel attack, various authorized troop movements which were apparently misinterpreted, and a statement the previous day by Col. Reynaldo Cabauatan, who had been in hiding since dismissal from the Army after the January coup attempt, that he was setting up a "nationalist provisional government".

Government troops were deployed around the Malacanang Palace on October 6, in what was officially termed as a "dress rehearsal". Twenty soldiers and civilians were arrested on the same day, including an army colonel. There were widespread reports at this time that a new coup was being planned, involving Honasan, Cabauatan, the "Guardians" military fraternity, politicians from the right-wing Grand Alliance for Democracy and former associates of President Marcos. Security outside the palace was heavily reinforced on October 16, amid reports that rebel soldiers were planning to assassinate the President during a rally organized by labour groups in support of wage demands. On October 18, troops and tanks again surrounded the palace after a soldier linked to Cabauatan stole an armoured vehicle from Fort Bonifacio, leading to fears that a new coup was under way. The car was later recovered with a flag of the Guardians in it.

Rumours that martial law was about to be declared were repeatedly denied by the government; however, in a significant shift of position, Aquino said on October 12 that there would be no martial law "unless it is absolutely necessary; unless it is for the greater good of the country". This was the first occasion on which she had stopped short of an outright rejection of such a step.

In an expensive attempt to meet some of the grievances of the armed forces, and thereby buy their loyalty, the Senate on October 23 approved a series of pay increases for military personnel. The monthly rate for private soldiers would be increased from US$23 to $48, and that of generals from $357 to $550.

In the wake of the coup attempt, President Aquino's government began to take on an increasingly embattled aspect. On September 9, Aquino demanded the resignation of the entire Cabinet, to allow her complete freedom to make new appointments. She had been faced with persistent public criticism of her administration, and recent attacks had focused in particular on Joker Arroyo, her Executive Secretary, and Teodoro Locsin, the Presidential Counsel. Only the previous day, Arroyo, a former human rights lawyer, had been accused in Congress of being anti-military and pro-communist, as well as being criticized for disorganization, inefficiency and manipulating the President, and, together with Locsin, of having a brash and abrasive style.

The Cabinet was reappointed with five significant changes on September 17. In addition to Arroyo and Locsin, other Ministers who lost their jobs included Salvador Laurel, Foreign Secretary and Vice-President; Jaime Ongpin, Finance Secretary; and Jose Fernandez, Central Bank Governor, whose dismissal had been expected since he was currently facing investigation with regard to alleged corruption during the later years of the Marcos regime.

Laurel, who retained the elective post of Vice-President, had increasingly distanced himself from the administration. He had recently made a tour of military bases, ostensibly to gauge the attitudes of the armed forces in the wake of the attempted coup, but which was reported to have been more of an attempt to encourage disaffection among the troops and to build a personal following. On September 16, Laurel complained that Aquino had no clear-cut policies to combat the NPA insurgency and accused the government of containing communist sympathizers. He also claimed that the President had reneged on an agreement made when he agreed to be her running-mate in the 1986 presidential elections whereby she undertook to allow him to appoint one-third of the government. Claiming to have been ignored in the decision-making process, Laurel announced on September 16 that he no longer wished to remain as Foreign Secretary.

Jaime Ongpin was found dead in his home on December 7, the fatal injury caused by a single shot to the head from a pistol found at his side. The death was widely, although not universally, regarded as suicide. As Finance Secretary, Ongpin had led debt rescheduling negotiations with the country's creditors. Earlier, as a member of the informal anti-Marcos "convenor group" in 1986, he had played a key role in urging Aquino to stand for President.

New members of the Cabinet appointed on September 17 included Arroyo's former deputy, Catalino Macaraig, as Executive Secretary, Vincente Jayme as Finance Secretary and Raul Manglapus as Foreign Secretary. Manglapus had opposed the presence of US bases in the Philippines during the Marcos regime, and his appointment at this time was seen as particularly significant, given the fact that the lease agreement on the US bases was due for renegotiation in 1989.

The day before the new Cabinet was appointed, Aquino answered crticisms embodied in a report given to her by Laurel on the armed forces grudges by repeating that her declared policy was to pursue war against the NPA and that she expected the Army to go on the offensive. She also insisted on the need to respect democratic practices, and to take economic measures to remove the root causes of the insurgency. On October 1, Aquino denied categorically that there were any communist sympathizers in her government. A list compiled by Laurel of 150 members of the administration, including 20 congressmen, was submitted to a closed congressional committee session on September 29 and was found to consist mainly of former opponents of Marcos, none of whom could legitimately be regarded as radicals.

The growing influence of Gen. Ramos in the government was confirmed in January 1988 when he took over the post of Defence

Minister from Rafael Ileto. Ileto had on a number of occasions criticized the armed forces leadership for its failure to overcome the threat from the communist insurgents.

THE THREAT FROM THE LEFT AND THE MOSLEM SEPARATISTS

The NPA challenge

Despite periodic efforts to renew negotiations between the government and the National Democratic Front, the possibilities of a negotiated settlement receded during Aquino's second year, increasingly so in the aftermath of the August coup attempt, when the government came under pressure from the right-wing opposition to give the Army free rein in the counter-insurgency drive. Since the most serious threat to its existence appeared to come from the Right, the administration sought to appease its opponents by taking a tougher line towards the Left in general and the New People's Army in particular.

Militarily, the NPA remained as a real threat to the government. Estimated to number between 24,000 and 30,000, to enjoy the support of one-quarter of the population and to control about one-fifth of rural territory (albeit in isolated pockets spread over a wide area), it stepped up its rural campaign over the year, particularly after the congressional elections and the August coup attempt. Meanwhile, the guerrillas' "sparrow squads" continued to stage hit-and-run attacks on policemen, officials and right-wing vigilante activists in Manila and other urban areas. Some of the attacks on policemen which were attributed to the NPA by the government and the media were in fact thought to be the work of street criminals or gangsters in search of weapons who masqueraded as guerrillas.

In a televised statement on February 28, 1987, President Aquino unveiled a new scheme designed to encourage guerrillas to surrender their weapons in return for an unconditional amnesty together with a financial reward and the promise of training for future employment.

The programme, which it was estimated would cost over US$50,000,000, was to last for six months and was to include the establishment of national rehabilitation centres throughout the country. Although the programme was condemned by the NPA's leadership as "a desperate bribe" on the part of the government, Gen. Ileto claimed that by the end of May some 4,000 rebels and associated activists (including

1,000 full-time NPA fighters) had taken advantage of the terms offered in the package. In practice however, many of those who attended surrender ceremonies, lured by various material incentives, were defined merely as "supporters" of the insurgency. After a total of 2,500 "communists" were recorded as surrendering in Bislig, Mindanao, on August 6, military spokesmen admitted that only 206 were communist guerrillas as such. Cash incentives to the surrendering "rebels" included $450 for each M-16 rifle handed over, and $275 for each Kalashnikov AK-47.

The announcement of the programme was followed by government initiatives to enter into negotiations with regional and local commanders of NPA units in an effort to exploit the divisions alleged to exist within the movement with regard to its response to the Aquino administration. An offer by the NPA's central leadership to resume talks at national level (with the proviso that the agenda should include "the roots of the conflict") was rejected by the government on March 5, on the grounds that satisfactory progress was being made in the local negotiations.

Anti-communist vigilante groups such as the Mindanao-based *Alsa Massa* (Masses Arise), which was committed to killing suspected communists or members of the NPA, continued to grow during 1987, often under the patronage of army officers. Several members of the government, particularly the Secretary for Local Government, Jaime Ferrer, were also known to support such organizations as instruments in the struggle against communist insurgency. Overall, there were estimated to be some 130 organizations, most of them locally based and funded by private landowners or businessmen, often with the support of local officials and army commanders.

On March 16, President Aquino ordered the disbanding of all vigilante organizations in line with the provisions of the new constitution, but in a speech on March 29 she revised this position and expressed her support for unarmed groups such as *Nakasaka* (People United for Peace) as part of a general campaign to resist communist infiltration. It was reported on June 8 that Ferrer had ordered all "officers in charge" (i.e. local government office holders appointed to replace Marcos supporters pending local elections) in the Bicol region to form vigilante groups to prevent the spread of communism in the area.

Ferrer's outspoken advocacy for expanding the role of the vigilante movements led to numerous threats against his life from the NPA, and on August 2 he was shot dead near his home in Manila by three assassins, presumed to be sparrow squad members.

As the year wore on, the vigilantes grew in strength and influence. In June, a new grouping called the "Association of Democratic Vigilantes and Concerned Entrepreneurs" was formed in Manila with the aim of identifying sparrow squad hideouts, while another armed group, the "Manila Crusaders for Peace and Democracy" was formed under police supervision in Manila. Left-wing activists from legal organizations were increasingly the target of attacks by vigilante groups, carried out with the apparent acquiescence of the Army.

In one of the most blatant such attacks, Leandro Alejandro, 27, general secretary of the left-wing *Bayan* New Nationalist Alliance), was shot dead in the Quezon City area of Manila on September 19. Alejandro had formerly been a prominent left-wing student leader; he had played a key role in organizing the August transport strike. He was killed on returning from a press conference at which he had proposed a general strike to protest against the increasing militarization of the Aquino administration. At Alejandro's funeral on September 29, *Bayan* supporters staged the year's biggest rally of protest against Aquino, during which they chanted slogans denouncing the "US-Aquino dictatorship" and its "creeping militarization". The event passed off peacefully after police and troops were given strict orders to show maximum tolerance.

Although Alejandro's killers were never identified, it was widely believed that his death resulted from an Army-sponsored crack-down on legal left-wing groups, which had forced many leftist activists to go underground. Alejandro's murder followed that of the KMU leader, Rolando Olalia, in November 1986, and a more recent assassination attempt on Bernabe Buscayno, the alleged founder of the NPA. All three men had been instrumental in setting up *Bayan* in 1985.

The NPA's military campaign escalated sharply in the wake of the right-wing oposition's August coup attempt, as it sought to exploit the confusion within the military to stage a number of operations. At the time of the mutiny, the Communist Party central committee promised that it would take "full advantage" of strains between the government and the military, claiming that this "open war among the reactionaries" would do nothing to "stem the surging revolutionary tide".

During August, the NPA scored a number of successes in the narrow Bicol peninsula, south-east of Manila. At its narrowest point, Bicol was linked to the rest of Luzon only by one road and a railway track. The NPA succeeded in cutting these lines of communication on several occasions, with a total of four bridges and eight electricity pylons being blown up during September alone. In response, the government sent two élite Scout Ranger battalions to the region in September, to reinforce the several thousand soldiers and constabulary stationed there. In a major show of strength on September 20, several hundred NPA guerrillas hijacked a Manila-bound train in Camarines Norte province, riding it to a nearby town where they attacked police outposts and the town hall. On October 6, the military spokesmen announced that a major NPA base at Sorgoson (in the peninsula) had been captured from the guerrillas.

The NPA also experienced victories in the Cagayan valley area of northern Luzon and in Quezon province in early September. On

September 13, however, the Army claimed to have captured NPA positions at San Juan, in Bataan province, near the capital. The guerrillas' successes were acknowledged by Gen. Ramos, the Chief of Staff, on September 22, when he admitted that military casualties had increased by 40 per cent since the coup attempt.

Buoyed up by these successes, the National Democratic Front (the political wing of the NPA) responded to efforts by members of the "legal left" to establish a broad anti-militarist consensus by offering on October 13 to reopen negotiations with the government. NDF spokesmen said that they were ready to co-operate with any political group in order to frustrate "US intervention and fascist attempts to impose a more repressive rule in this country". The government failed to respond to this initiative, and two weeks later, the insurgency war took on a new and potentially far-reaching dimension.

Three US servicemen, one of them retired, together with a Filipino civilian, were killed in separate attacks near the Clark Air Base on October 28. The killings were widely seen as the work of sparrow squads; responsibility was claimed the following day by the "Alex Boncayao Brigade" (named after a dead NPA leader), which warned that a total of 10 Americans would be killed in protest at the delivery the previous week of 10 US armoured personnel carriers to the Philippines Army for use in anti-insurgency operations.

Other reports however said that the NPA had denied responsibility, and suggested that the killings might have been the work of right-wing activists seeking to destabilize the government.

In the wake of the first American fatalities in the Philippines since 1974, security at all US installations was immediately tightened; restrictions were placed on all travel outside the bases, and off-base excursions for shopping and entertainment were banned. The restrictions had a devastating effect on the local economy of areas around the bases, with many shops and, particularly, bars being forced to close.

In a statement which appeared to represent a major shift of policy, the NDF announced on November 6 that US personnel, both military and civilian, were to be considered legitimate targets. The statement, signed by Satur Ocampo, the NDF's secretary-general, warned that the USA would "pay a high price" in terms of lives and property for its "political-military intervention" and "meddling" in the Philippines. This policy was reiterated in an NDF statement on January 8 which defined legitimate NPA targets as including "US imperialist advisers, troops, agents and business empires".

Following the October attacks, 39 presumed members of sparrow squads were arrested during a raid on November 1 on the Polytechnic University of the Philippines and the surrounding area in Manila, while 585 young men were rounded up for "character verification". The raid, which was carried out with President Aquino's approval, met with sustained press criticism, particularly over the use of hooded informers to identify suspects, which was condemned as being reminiscent of procedures used by Japanese occupation forces. A spokesman for the security forces subsequently admitted that this procedure should not have been adopted, and added that the conduct of raids was under review.

The NPA stepped up attacks on military bases in January 1988, engaging in major battles on January 27 with army units at Santa Ana (close to Clark Air base). On the same day, in a speech marking Ramos's assumption of the post of Defence Secretary, President Aquino promised to allow the Army a free hand in prosecuting the war against the communists, adding that she wanted to see the insurgency crushed by the end of her presidential term. She dismissed allegations that the military had carried out atrocities as "total lies", and accused human rights monitoring groups of engaging in "worthless carping". Aquino promised the Army that she would "stand by you in thick and thin; to share the blame, defend your actions, and enjoy with you the final victory". The day after Aquino's speech, the Conference of Bishops voted to close down the Church's National Secretariat of Social Action, on the grounds that it had been infiltrated by NPA supporters. In a further example of the government's increasingly tough line against the Communists, Gen. Ramos, who had recently been appointed Defence Secretary, announced on February 2 that the amnesty offer to NPA guerrillas would cease to apply from the end of the month. In response to army officers' appeals, President Aquino announced on March 23 the disbandment of the Regional Unified Command structure. Field commanders had frequently complained that the structure hamstrung their operational ability, since it effectively meant that all major strategic decisions had to be referred back to Manila for authorization. Its abolition would allow individual commanders greater scope for initiative in the field, and, according to some reports, reduce the level of direct political influence over their decisions.

The Army claimed on February 5 that 20 leading communist activists, including two CPP central committee members and four "sparrow squad" leaders, had been arrested in a sweep on guerrilla hideouts in Manila. According to Gen. de Villa (the newly-appointed Chief of Staff), the arrests had "broken the communists' communication nerve centre in Manila", and would "create a major disruption in the insurgency".

As part of the government's effort to undermine support for the NPA in the mountainous Cordillera area to the north of Manila, President Aquino signed a decree in July 1987 to establish the Cordillera Administrative Region for the 1,000,000 tribal inhabitants living there.

A 250-member interim executive board and regional assembly, with limited powers and a small budget, were created pending the negotiation of an agreement on full autonomy which would be presented to the Congress and then to the inhabitants of the region in a referendum. The interim administration was reported to include Fr Conrado Balweg, the leader of the Cordillera People's Liberation Army (CPLA), which had broken from the NPA in April 1986 and had signed a separate peace with the Aquino government in September of that year. In the weeks prior to the presidential decree several detachments of government troops had been sent to the region to provide support for Fr Balweg in his struggle against the NPA and the newly formed communist Cordillera People's Democratic Front, both of which were committed to the destruction of the CPLA. One of the principal tribal leaders in the Cordillera, Daniel Ngayaan, was murdered by CPLA gunmen in early October. Ngayaan had played a leading role in efforts to secure recognition for tribal people's rights in the region.

The Moslem dimension

The optimism which had surrounded President Aquino's early talks with Moslem rebels fighting for self-rule in the south of the country gave way to recrimination and deadlock during her second year in office, with neither side able to agree on a formula for autonomy to end the 16-year long Moslem rebellion. Hopes for a settlement had been raised as a result of a truce agreed in January between the government and the rival Moslem secessionist movements — the Moro National Liberation Front (MNLF — the strongest of the three), the Bangsa Moro National Liberation Front (BMNLF) and the Moro Islamic Liberation Front (MILF). All three groups were invited to attend peace talks, and, while the MNLF and BMNLF accepted, the MILF persistently refused to do so, adding that it would not recognize any agreement to which it was not a party. Prospects brightened when the MNLF, the strongest rebel force, agreed in February 1987 to drop demands for an independent Moslem homeland and accepted instead a proposal for "full autonomy". Negotiations, however, ran onto difficult ground soon after.

One of the major sticking points was the new constitution endorsed in a national plebiscite on February 11, which called for full autonomy for Moslem areas in the south where this was supported by a referendum; in effect confining autonomy to about five provinces with a Moslem majority. The MNLF rejected these limitations, arguing that self-rule should extend to all traditional Moslem areas, even where migration had created a Christian majority. This wider area included Mindanao, and the islands of Sulu, Basia, Palawan and Tawi-Tawi.

MNLF negotiators reiterated these wider territorial claims by proposing on February 20 that President Aquino use her executive powers to create a "Bangsa Moro Autonomous Region" (BMAR) covering 23 provinces. According to foreign commentators, the MNLF was concerned that the new Congress, due to meet in July, would be hostile to any real devolution of power to autonomous governments. The government's chief negotiator, Emmanuel Pelaez — who was also the country's ambassador to Washington — refused, however, to move beyond the position outlined in the constitution. A further session of talks was held on March 12 at which the MNLF's chief negotiator, Habib Hashim, threatened to renew the war if a settlement was not reached without delay.

In early April, a series of incidents involving government soldiers and Moslem rebels led to the MNLF suspending the negotiations. On April 6, government forces were reported to have attacked a rebel base in Zamboanga del Sur province in what was the first major clash between the two sides since the ceasefire signed in September 1986. There were further reports of fighting on April 8 when 10 Moslem rebels were killed by government troops in Bukidnon.

However, in mid-April, the MNLF abruptly softened their negotiating stance. They dropped their demand for a 23-province autonomous region and proposed instead immediate self-rule for 13 provinces. Autonomy for the other 10 would be subject to a plebiscite — a move which implicitly recognized that these provinces might not accept incorporation into a Moslem homeland. Pelaez welcomed the shift as a "breath of fresh air", but after two days of talks with President Aquino, he told the MNLF that the government would not alter its negotiating position.

Talks remained deadlocked when the two sides met again, just prior to the Congressional elections on May 11. Frustrated by the stalemate, the MNLF's leader, Nur Misuari, threatened on May 4 that MNLF troops would destroy foreign plantations if demands for regional autonomy were not met. Two days later, government negotiators made the surprise announcement that agreement had been reached with the Moslem rebels on forming a joint commission to draft an autonomy package for Mindanao. Since talks collapsed immediately afterwards, foreign observers viewed the announcement as a ploy to give the impression that talks were making progress before the Congressional elections.

The breakdown of the talks coincided with the abduction on May 5 of two Swiss nationals working for the Red Cross in southern Mindanao. Both were eventually released unharmed, though one was held for three weeks. Military officials ruled out the involvement of Moslem separatists, but there was speculation that a splinter group, the Moro Islamic Liberation Front (MILF), had staged the kidnapping to draw attention to its exclusion from the autonomy negotiations.

There was an attempt to revive the peace process in early June, when the MNLF called for talks in Saudi Arabia under the aegis of the Islamic

Conference Organization. The government, however, rejected the proposal. On June 8, the press secretary, Teodoro Benigno, said the President did not want to bring an international dimension to what was a purely domestic problem.

With the peace talks stalled, there was concern in government circles that Moslem rebels might renew their military activities at a time when government forces were involved in operations against the communist guerillas on Mindanao. In the magazine *Asia Week*, on July 19, Ambassador Pelaez was reported as saying that should the two groups form a tactical alliance (as they had in the past) the government would be hard put to fight on several fronts.

As part of its campaign against the NPA, the military authorities had encouraged the formation of several vigilante groups, including the Mindanao Christian Liberation Army (CLA) whose activities were first reported in June. Foreign observers saw official encouragement of the group as an attempt to renew tensions between the Christian and Moslem communities on Mindanao and weaken the case for Moslem autonomy.

On July 21, a week before the new Philippines Congress met, President Aquino made a bold move to revive the peace process. She proposed to establish, by Presidential decree, a "regional executive" to govern 10 provinces, formed by merging two largely symbolic autonomous regions set up by President Marcos after the signing of the 1976 Tripoli agreement. An 11-member council would supervise the region which would have wide financial powers, including, for example, control over the Southern Philippines Development Agency. The decree also provided for a security force to assist in the defence of the region, which government sources saw as a new role for the MNLF forces. According to foreign observers, President Aquino felt she had gone as far as she could in creating a homeland for the MNLF, without interfering with the congress's constitutional mandate to pass an act of autonomy creating a more limited Moslem Mindanao.

The plan was discussed by both sides at a meeting in Jeddah on July 23, where the MNLF came under pressure from some of its supporters in the Islamic Conference Organization (including officials from Malaysia, Pakistan and Saudi Arabia) to accept President Aquino's proposals. The MNLF, however, refused to be swayed and rejected the plan on the grounds that the decree restricted autonomy to only 10 provinces, less than the 13 envisaged under the Tripoli agreement; and because of a clause insisting that a plebiscite would have to be a precondition of formal autonomy.

Following the failure of the Jeddah talks, there were reports in the major national dailies that Nur Misuari had instructed his forces to stage offensives against government forces. On August 5, Maj.-Gen. Cesar Tapia, chief of the Army's Southern Command based in Mindanao, issued a tough warning that the Army was prepared for "all-out war" against Moslem insurgents should they start attacking military installations.

On August 20, a new peace initiative was launched by the government when Ambassador Pelaez returned to Washington, and was replaced as chief negotiator by the Health Secretary, Alfredo Bengzon. Bengzon offered to break the month-long deadlock with new talks. Little substantial progress was achieved, however, and while the armed conflict remained at a relatively low level, it seemed likely that, two years after the people's power revolution, Moslem separatist demands would remain a thorn in the side of the Manila government for some time to come.

THE ECONOMIC CONTEXT

The decline under Marcos

When the euphoria of the people's power revolution had subsided, the new government was faced with the task of reconstructing the country's economy, weakened by the twin scourges of world recession and corrupt mismanagement.

For much of Marcos's reign, the Philippines had enjoyed a booming economy. During the 1970s gross national product (GNP) had increased by an average of 7 per cent per year. The high growth rate, however, masked a number of structural defects in the economy. The government's emphasis on high levels of investment aimed at rapid industrialization led to substantial trade deficits due to the level of imports of producer goods and increasingly expensive oil supplies. These undercut the overall aim of the strategy, which was to achieve sustained growth via import substitution. Philippines industry was protected against overseas competition by high tariff barriers, which helped to conceal inefficient manufacturing methods, and was heavily supported by foreign finance, easily available during most of the decade.

The inherent weaknesses of the economy emerged at the turn of the decade, when world recession rapidly reduced the amount of foreign finance available. The majority of such loans as were made were shorter term and higher interest. Together with other factors, including the emergence of rival producers, the recession reduced demand for the Philippines' traditional commodity exports, particularly sugar, coconut oil, timber and copper. Consequently, as its capacity to earn foreign exchange was reduced, the Philippines' ability to service its rapidly rising debt bill was placed under increasing strain. To some extent, the decline in the commodity export sector was offset by a growth in "new" export industries, notably processed foods and drinks, electrical components and finished garments. These "new" exports accounted for 71 per cent of the country's visible foreign earnings in 1985, compared with 19 per cent a decade earlier.

In an effort to halt the decline, the government announced a number of austerity measures from 1982 onwards, including cutbacks in state expenditure and the introduction of a flexible exchange rate. Together with tax reforms, these resulted in the halving of the budget deficit, from 4.3 per cent of GNP in 1982 to 2 per cent the following year. The economic crisis intensified from 1983 onwards, however, with the spiralling foreign debt equivalent to 73 per cent of GNP by the end of the year. After the assassination of Benigno Aquino in August 1983, investor confidence hit a new low, resulting in high levels of capital outflow and a steady slide in the value of the peso against the US dollar, from P8 = $1 in 1981 to P19 = $1 in 1985. Real GNP fell by 6.8 per cent in 1984, while rapidly rising inflation, fuelled by the growth in money supply, reached a high of 65 per cent per annum at the end of the year.

In support of further austerity measures, the International Monetary Fund agreed a major standby credit of 615,000,000 special drawing rights (equivalent to about US$600,000,000) in December 1984. The IMF agreement followed in the wake of rescheduling agreements with both the "Paris Club" of Western creditor nations and a syndicate of 483 commercial bank creditors.

Although the government succeeded in reducing inflation to 23 per cent in 1985, the belt-tightening measures in general merely exacerbated the stagnation of the economy, reducing domestic demand and encouraging the flight of capital. Economic vitality was further stymied by high interest rates, which were running as high as 40 per cent at the beginning of the year. Manufacturing activity declined by 14 per cent during 1985, while construction fell by over 45 per cent over the same period. Overall, GNP fell again by 3.8 per cent during the year. As measured in 1972 pesos, real GNP per capita had fallen from a peak of P1,939 in 1981 to P1,897 in 1983 and P1,640 in 1985. Allowing for the peso's slide against the dollar over this period, these values are equivalent to $245 in 1981, $174 in 1983 and $88 in 1985. At the time of the change of regime, industry was estimated to be operating at below 50 per cent capacity.

The depression was exacerbated by the rising tide of "cronyism", in which President Marcos and his close friends and relatives grew fabulously rich through a mixture of blatant corruption and personal, monopolistic control of key companies and state enterprises. Proceeds which could have been reinvested in the industries concerned instead went straight into the pockets of a few individuals, further impoverishing the economy and limiting the potential for fresh investment.

Aquino's new broom — prospects and problems

After establishing itself in power, the Aquino administration announced a series of reforms as part of a medium-term development strategy designed to "alleviate poverty, generate more productive employment and promote equity and social justice". In practice, the programme was aimed at restoring internal and international confidence in the economy, and at revitalizing it by removing the corruption and cronyism of the old regime.

The new government ordered the dismantling of the crony-dominated monopolies that had controlled the sugar, coconut, grain, meat and other industries. One of the first direct consequences of this was the removal of the ban on the export of copra (a coconut product). The government also encouraged diversification away from traditional plantation crops towards new enterprises such as prawn culture, which were less vulnerable to world market price fluctuations. A privatization programme involving some 125 state corporations was embarked upon, and the "Presidential Commission on Good Government" was set up to oversee the recovery of assets illicitly acquired by the Marcos family and its "crony" associates.

This proved to be a very slow process; by August 2, 1987, (the deadline laid down in the constitution) the government had filed 35 cases seeking civil damages of over $90,000 million against Marcos, his wife, and nearly 300 others. These included Enrile, Gen. Fabian Ver (former Chief of Staff), Benjamin "Kokoy" Romualdez (Imelda Marcos's brother, a former ambassador and provincial governor), Eduardo Cojuangco (a cousin of Imelda and also former governor), Edgardo Angara (a senator and former president of the University of the Philippines) and Roberto Benedicto (former ambassador to Japan and president of the Philippines National Bank). The levels of cronyism reached staggering proportions: "Kokoy", for example, had held an absolute monopoly of the coconut industry, shares in 243 companies, and was reputed to own 184 properties.

Damages were being sought for suffering caused to the Filipino people, breach of trust and abuse of power, and various acts of corruption. Ramon Diaz, the chairman of the Presidential Commission on Good Government, estimated that Ferdinand Marcos and his family were worth some 2,000 billion pesos. The new constitution, however, required the accused to appear in court to answer charges; most of the accused were abroad and President Aquino had stated on a number of occasions that Marcos himself would not be allowed to return until the political situation had stabilized.

In an effort to stimulate the domestic economy, the government cut interest rates and lowered fuel prices, resulting in a drop in the cost of basic foods and consumer goods. A number of tax reforms were introduced, reducing the burden on agricultural and industrial production, as well as removing some of the tax exemptions and incentives that had been abused under the previous regime. A series of key appointments were made to state financial organizations, the customs and revenue, as part of the drive to eliminate the corruption which had characterized the Marcos administration.

In an attempt both to alleviate rural poverty and boost consumer demand, the new administration launched a "Community Employment Development Programme" (CEDP), with a budget of P4,000 million in 1986 and P9,000 million in 1987. The programme aimed to create jobs through labour-intensive projects to improve local infrastructure, such as rural feeder roads, irrigation, water supplies, reforestation, seed production and distribution and small ports. By the end of 1987, the CEDP was planned to have created 1,000,000 jobs. In practice, however, this figure was thought likely to be an overestimate. In an effort to ensure the correct running of the scheme, the government requested local development organizations to monitor the progress of the programme. Some of these reported various irregularities, including projects abandoned before completion or those that had become subject to corruption.

Further revitalization measures included the progressive removal of import controls on some 1,200 products, and the establishment of an "Omnibus Investment Code" to attract foreign investment at favourable terms. The government also launched a "debt-to-equity swap" initiative, in which commercial creditors would be offered the opportunity of transforming debt into equity investment through the issue of non-interest-bearing certificates, denominated in US dollars and available at discount rates. The certificates could be redeemed at face value in pesos only, on condition that the money was invested in the Philippines in government-approved enterprises.

The new government's long-term objectives were enshrined in a development plan covering the period 1987-92, which predicted an annual growth in real GNP of 6.5 per cent, with per capita GNP rising by 4 per cent per year. Investment was planned to grow at a rate of 10 per cent annually, with exports and imports both set to increase by about 7 per cent per annum. Over the whole period, the government hoped to cut the number of unemployed from 12 per cent to 5 per cent of the workforce, and the number of "underemployed" from 33 per cent to 24 per cent. The plan also aimed to reduce the proportion of Filipino families living below the official poverty line from the present estimate of 70 per cent to 45 per cent. The development plan emphasized the importance of the agricultural sector, which had been neglected as a result of the Marcos regime's industrialization drive.

The government's policies received a seal of approval from the IMF which agreed a new aid package of 422,100,000 special drawing rights (equivalent to about $513,000,000) in July 1986. Of the total, SDR198,000,000 was to be made available over the following 18-month period in standby credit, and SDR224,100,000 was to be made available under the IMF's compensatory financing facility for an export shortfall in the 12 months ending June 1986. (The seventh and final tranche of the December 1984 IMF aid agreement—see above—had been suspended in April after the change of regime.) After protracted negotiations, the "Paris Club" of 14 Western creditor nations agreed to a major reorganization of loan repayments in January 1987. Agreement on rescheduling and restructuring of debt payments to the country's 483 commercial bank creditors was reached in March of that year, although subsequent disagreements over interest rates and the government's wish to make "debt-to-equity" swaps compulsory delayed the implementation of the deal, and provoked calls by the Philippines Congress for "selective repudiation" of some of the debts. At the end of 1986, the Philippines' total external debt was estimated as $28,617 million, making it the tenth biggest debtor in the world.

In part thanks to the incoming government's policies, and in part due to external factors, the Philippines economy experienced a significant turnround during 1986, not least as a result of renewed investor confidence. The stock market, which had been virtually moribund during the closing years of the Marcos regime, was the scene of considerable activity, with its index rising from 131 at the start of the year to 425 at the close. Real GNP grew by 0.13 per cent over the year (the first net growth since 1983), while inflation was reduced to less than 2 per cent. Interest rates averaged only 10 per cent by the end of the year. The recovery was aided by rising prices on the world market for the country's traditional commodities, which accounted for two-thirds of export earnings during 1986 (compared to less than one-fifth in 1985 — see above), contributing to a trade surplus of $17,000,000 — the first since 1973.

Despite these signs of recovery, serious problems remained for the economy as a whole. Investment remained low, and the burden of foreign debt would continue to act as a severe strain on the country's financial resources. Commodity exports remained under threat from price fluctuations and from overseas competition, while prices for the newer exports of electrical goods and clothing had failed to increase as hoped. Continuing low industrial productivity, and a long-standing failure to give adequate support to the agriculture sector, threatened the future prospects for sustained economic growth. A further problem facing the government was labour relations. In the first few months in power, the government, and particularly the Labour Minister, Augusto Sanchez, supported trade unions in their right to strike. A record number of disputes took place in 1986, as unions fought to recover wage levels that had been severely damaged by the previous two years' inflation. During late 1986 and 1987, however, the government took a harder line, partly in response to the large number of strikes, and partly in line with its general shift to the right in an attempt to placate the growing military and conservative opposition. Sanchez was dismissed, and increasing restrictions placed on unions, while labour activists became subject to intimidation and, on occasion, assassination.

The highest single economic hurdle for the government, however, was agrarian reform, on which it had staked its credibility, and which formed the principal plank of its strategy to defeat the threat from the communist guerrillas.

LAND REFORM — DEBATES AND DELAYS

Both during her election campaign, and after coming to power as President, Mrs Aquino had made much of the need for a major redistribution of agricultural land. Aside from the powerful humanitarian arguments in favour of such a move, the essential appeal of land reform to the government was threefold. First, it was believed that it would decisively undercut the level of support among rural communities for the New People's Army guerrillas. Second, it was hoped to encourage agricultural diversification away from loss-making export crops such as sugar and coconut, and finally, it was seen as helping to stimulate domestic demand by raising rural incomes and thereby breaking the cycle of chronic underconsumption which characterized the country's economy.

The fact that the government had failed to act decisively on the issue during its first year in power was attributed to its reluctance to alienate the owners of large plantations, who had traditionally wielded a considerable degree of political influence, and also to its desire that the matter be decided by a democratically-elected legislature rather than by means of executive decree. The Cabinet itself was sharply divided over the scale and timing of any reform, with left-leaning and liberal members favouring genuine, sweeping redistribution, while conservative ministers preferred a more restrained, gradual approach that would allow most landowners to retain the majority of their holdings.

Some limited land reforms had been carried out during Ferdinand Marcos's presidency under a scheme which was set up in 1973. The plan only affected holdings of over seven hectares of rice and maize, which in total amounted to some 600,000 ha. By 1986, some 300,000 ha. were officially said to have been distrubuted to about 200,000 beneficiaries, although there were conflicting reports as to how thoroughly the redistribution had been implemented.

A more ambitious scheme had been suggested in 1986 by Daniel Lacson, the Governor of Negros Occidental, one of the provinces most affected by the decline in the world sugar trade. Over Negros as a whole, which produced 60 per cent of the country's sugar crop, thousands of sugar plantation workers had been reduced from an already marginal existence to one of absolute destitution, with many dying through the effects of prolonged malnutrition. Under Lacson's scheme, 60 per cent of the existing plantation lands would remain under sugar, while 30 per cent would be converted to other uses and the remaining 10 per cent woud be allocated to the sugar workers to enable them to grow their own food crops. The principal plantation workers' union, the National Federation of Sugar Workers (NFSW), had already begun to operate a "farmlots programme" on plantation land that was lying idle or was inappropriate for sugar cultivation. The plan was generally welcomed as a first step by the NFSW, but was strongly denounced by many landowners, who saw it as an attack on their rights and as a possible precursor to more far-reaching redistribution. Vigilante groups funded by the planters had already taken action against the NFSW's farmlots, murdering union activists and destroying the crops in some areas. Such actions were also carried out by members of the armed forces, many of whose senior officers enjoyed close relations with the planters. Opposition from the landowners was seen as the reason behind President Aquino's failure to issue an executive decree instituting the "60-30-10" programme, as it was known, during a visit to the province in October 1986.

The government was eventually stirred into action on land reform by the public outcry over the Mendiola Bridge incident and the breakdown of the ceasefire agreement with the NPA (see above). On February 8, 1987, a land reform programme was hastily outlined by Heherson Alverez, the then Minister for Agrarian Reform. Consisting of four stages, the programme was to run for five years, with 5,400,000 hectares of land being redistributed in the first three years of its operation.

Stage one was essentially concerned with the completion of the redistribution process provided for in the Marcos plan (see above). A total of 400,000 tenants were expected to benefit in this phase. Stage two envisaged the distribution of 939,000 hectares of land which had either been abandoned or seized by the government from the supporters of Marcos who were deemed to have acquired it illegitimately. This stage was anticipated to affect some 670,000 tenants. The significant parts of the programme were contained in stages three and four. Stage three dealt with the break-up of 1,500,000 ha. of private sugar and coconut plantations, while stage four would enshrine access rights to and changes in the use of public land, and would also provide for improved agricultural extension assistance. Both these stages would require congressional legislation. Overall, the draft programme envisaged settling 3,400,000 peasant farmers as on 7,400,000 ha. Mr Alverez stressed that legitimate owners of land would be compensated for their loss; 10 per cent of the total compensation would be by a cash payment, while the remainder would take the form of government bonds, maturing over 10 years at a rate of 10 per cent every year. Although Alverez did not give any indication of the total cost of the programme, unofficial estimates suggested that this could be upwards of $5,000 million.

LAND REFORM — DEBATES AND DELAYS

At a press conference on March 3 the President announced that as a first step towards financing the land reform programme the government would sell some 400 companies (many of them bankrupt) which it had expropriated from supporters of Marcos.

Questioned about the future of the Hacienda Luisita sugar estate of the Cojuangco family (into which Mrs Aquino had been born), the President stated that her brothers and sisters would "abide by any laws that are enacted". It was believed that the President owned only a small share of the 6,000-hectare estate, situated in Tarlac province 50 miles north of Manila, whose estimated 20,000 inhabitants had incomes which were twice the national average.

Reaction from landowners was generally hostile, and this became more so after President Aquino promised on May 29 to begin the initial stages of the land programme prior to the inauguration of Congress in July. Groups of plantation owners threated to withdraw bank deposits, to refuse to pay taxes and to undertake mass protests if the reform programme was implemented. A large demonstration of Negros planters gathered in the provincial capital of Bacolod on June 6 and threatened to "fight for an independent Negros" if the reform programme went ahead. The planters' opposition to reform was strengthened by the fact that both sugar and coconut prices had recently begun to recover. In several provinces in Mindanao, notably Davao and Cotabato, some landowners declared that they would consider supporting the Moslem insurgency if the government decided to press ahead with the scheme. Across the whole country, landowners were taking precautionary measures such as dividing up estates between individual family members, to reduce the overall size.

The reform programme was criticized in other quarters as unworkable. A World Bank report warned that it would be very costly, involving "hard choices in the allocation of domestic and external resources". The Bank added that it could "severely strain the government's institutional and administrative capacity". It also criticized as insubstantial the "various transitional voluntary land-sharing schemes" suggested by the government as an interim measure for the early stages of the reform programme. One of the main criticisms of the programme was its division into stages, with the most important phases coming last. Both the World Bank and other critics warned that interminable delays might result as plantation owners fought to postpone the implementation of the programme.

The plan was also attacked by Vice-President Salvador Laurel, who termed it a "shotgun solution" which would create a new class of dispossessed landowners awaiting government compensation payments.

In response to the criticisms, the government announced a new programme in the form of a presidential decree signed on July 21. The new "Comprehensive Agrarian Reform Programme" endorsed the principle of face-value compensation for landowners and low-interest credit for peasant beneficiaries, and approved initial funding of P2,500 million for the scheme. Compensation would be determined by the government on the basis of the owner's declaration of current market value. Coporate landowners woud be allowed to issue stocks to their workers in lieu of land.

Most significantly, the new plan specified that all public and private agricultural land would be liable for redistribution, with the exception of that used for defence, schools, and other public uses and the ancestral lands of indigenous communities. However, the decree charged Congress with the crucial tasks of determining within 90 days the timing of the redistribution and the minimum size of holdings to be affected. It also ruled that those who had seized land illegally since February 1986 would be rendered ineligible for inclusion within the scheme. This provision would have particularly serious consequences for self-help programmes such as the NFSW's farmlots project. In response to this, and to the fact that the landowner-dominated Congress was to have a major role in deciding the most important sections of the programme, the new measures were vehemently criticized by the left, which staged a number of demonstrations focusing on the Mendiola Bridge in Manila. According to the government, however, the programme would "directly provide economic benefits to a large number of the poorest and most disaffected members of our society, and thus contribute, more than any other policy measure, to the long-term stability of our country".

Congress failed to meet the 90-day deadline, with the reform programme coming in for strong criticism from many deputies, who suggested a number of amendments which would significantly reduce its impact. The government remained theoretically committed to the principle of land reform, with Aquino declaring at the beginning of 1988 that "we will persevere and we will succeed" in achieving "comprehensive" redistribution. Such declarations were not, however, accompanied by renewed action, and with the government still facing pressure from the right, many observers believed that land reform would be shelved for the foreseeable future, with disastrous consequences for the majority of the nation's impoverished rural populace.

THE AMERICAN PERSPECTIVE : A survey of the Aquino administration's relationship with its key ally.

When the US Ambassador to the Philippines, Stephen Bosworth, retired from his post on April 2, 1987, he was optimistic about the state of bilateral relations. Most problems, he said in an interview, fell into a daily management rather than a crisis category. The climate was to change abruptly in the next eight months with the murders of three US servicemen, the unprecedented recall of a US embassy official, and the resurgence of a strong anti-American Filipino nationalism.

President Aquino had paid a highly successful visit to Washington in September 1986, securing US$200,000,000 worth of aid commitments in addition to $150,000,000 approved earlier. The new package had been approved by Congress following an address by Mrs Aquino to a joint sitting of the Senate and House of Representatives.

At the start of 1987, the Reagan administration was mainly preoccupied by threats to the stability of the Aquino government, particularly the renewed problem of communist insurgency. President Aquino's decision to launch a military offensive against the NPA following the breakdown of a ceasefire agreement on February 8, had wide support in the US administration. There were promises of more US military aid, in contrast to the cutbacks in the latter days of the Marcos regime. In February, the Secretary of State, George Shultz, lobbied the American Congress to double US military aid to the Philippines in 1987 to US$100,000,000.

While the Reagan administration remained openly committed to a policy of unqualified support for Aquino, it became apparent that there were differences of opinion between the State Department and the Pentagon over her handling of the insurgency problem. The State Department was on the whole supportive of the government's attempts to revive the economy and establish political stability as part of a long-term strategy to defeat the communists. The Pentagon and CIA, on the other hand, wanted the counter-insurgency effort to be made the top priority and pushed strongly for more resources to be made available to the Philippines Army.

In late March, it was widely reported that President Reagan had secretly authorized the CIA to engage in covert operations against communist forces in the Philippines. One news report claimed the agency had permission to spend US$10,000,000 over a two-year period. According to intelligence sources, the CIA's expanded role was needed to rebuild the Philippines military-intelligence services, left demoralised and depleted by the departure of many Marcos loyalists. A visit to the Philippines in February by a team led by Maj.-Gen. (retd.) John Singlaub was widely reported to be part of this process. Singlaub was currently chairman of the World Anti-Communist League and was an old friend of Ferdinand Marcos. The CIA's new activities were attacked by US human rights activists. A group headed by the former US Attorney General, Ramsay Clark, which visited the Philippines in May, claimed that the CIA was organizing anti-communist groups such as the Alsa Massa and the Civilian Home Defence Force which had been accused of terrorising local populations. Philippine government officials denied the allegations, accusing the mission of interfering in the country's internal affairs.

Irritation in army and government circles over the CIA and Defence Department's criticism of the anti-communist campaign came to a head on March 19, when, in testimony to the US House of Representatives subcommittee on Asian and Pacific Affairs, Asst. Secretary of Defence Richard Armitage, attacked the Aquino government for failing to "develop a comprehensive counter-insurgency plan that integrates military, political, economic and social programmes". Armitage's criticism of the conduct of the war provoked an angry reaction. A group of mid-level officers met with President Aquino on March 20 to express their "deep resentment " and the President herself was described as being "peeved" by the remarks.

In the following weeks, Aquino began to criticize the United States openly for failing to deliver combat helicopters and medicine pledged during her visit to the USA in September 1986. On May 4, at a ceremony to mark the 51st anniversary of the Philippine Air Force, she attacked the delays, saying Washington should not expect Philippines troops to fight communist insurgency "with our teeth and our hands".

A delivery of 10 combat helicopters was made in early June, shortly before a visit by the US Secretary of State, George Shultz, on June 13-15. Speculation that the visit would lead to more financial aid proved unfounded. An agreement signed on June 15 to deliver $163,000,000 referred to aid already allocated for 1987. However, soon after the visit, on July 22, the US embassy in Manila announced that military aid to the Philippines for 1987 had been doubled to $100,000,000 to help counter-insurgency operations.

In the latter part of the year, the focus of attention was switched to a perennial bone of contention between the two countries; the US military presence in the Philippines. Under a 1983 agreement, talks were due to take place in 1988 on the question of US payment for the huge bases at Subic Bay and Clark Field. There were reports that many in the US government were pushing for the scope of the negotiations to be expanded into a full-scale review of the Military Bases Agreement even though this was not due to expire until 1991.

Both sides expected a round of hard bargaining, not least because the new civilian government could not ignore the long-standing public concern over the bases. The Far Eastern Economic Review described the changed atmosphere: "the Philippine press is freer; more Filipinos have become politicised by nationalist rhetoric opposing the foreign bases, and anxiety over nuclear weapons believed stored at the bases has increased in recent years. Most of all, a wide consensus now exists that the US is getting the bases too cheaply". Another concern was the discovery of AIDS among prostitutes associated with US servicemen. On May 24, the Philippines Health Secretary, Alfredo Bengzon, had asked the authorities at Subic Bay and Clark Field to take action to prevent the spread of the disease.

The new assertiveness on the bases issue was reflected in the new constitution ratified on February 2, which stated that any new bases agreement had to be approved by two-thirds of the Philippines Senate. The Senate could also put any new agreement to a national referendum. Another clause said the Philippines would pursue a policy of "freedom from nuclear weapons" in its territory. A nuclear ban would have seriously impaired the America's ability to operate out of the Philippines, but the Aquino administration side-stepped any potential confrontation by adopting a policy of not questioning whether US warships or planes were carrying nuclear weapons.

On August 30, the same day that the new US ambassador, Nicholas Platt, took up his post, a bill to ban nuclear weapons in the Philippines was introduced into the Senate by Senator Wigberto Tanada, a left-wing lawyer. It was co-sponsored by several moderate politicians close to Aquino. The bill outlawed the storage or possession of nuclear weapons or material; and forbade the transport of nuclear arms into the country as well as their transit through the country's air space and territorial waters. It was widely felt that the comprehensive nature of the bill, if passed, could result in the withdrawal of the US bases. However, most commentators saw the measure as a ploy to obtain leverage in the upcoming review of the bases agreement.

As talks on the bases loomed, American officials became deeply concerned in the autumn of 1987 by a growing anti-American sentiment. The public mood had begun to sour following rumours of American complicity in the attempted coup by rebel soldiers in August (see chapter 5).

It was in this highly charged atmosphere that on October 28, three US servicemen and a Filipino bystander were killed within 15 minutes of one another in separate incidents near the Clark Field Air Base (see chapter

6). This, and subsequent threats against US personnel by the NPA, served to focus attention on the presence of US forces close to Manila, and to their vulnerability to guerrilla attack, in the run-up to the negotiations on the bases.

Several American and Asian publications commented in November on a growing anti-American mood in the Philippines, particularly in Manila. Newsweek on November 17 quoted one Asian diplomat in the capital as saying: "in the love-hate relationship with America, the 'hate' part is getting the emphasis now". Against this background, it was not surprising that US interests came under attack. In early November, a row developed over armed patrols of US soldiers set up after the October shootings, to guard areas outside the two main US bases where American personnel lived. The former Defence Minister, Juan Ponce Enrile, attacked the government for permitting them, calling it an "insult to Philippine sovereignty". On November 10, the House of Representatives authorized a special investigation into the allegations of US involvement in the August mutiny; the same day the Senate approved the appointment of a special review committee, including leaders of both houses of Congress and Cabinet ministers, to make an urgent study of the need for a continued US military presence in the country. The wide-ranging review was to cover all military and security agreements, including the bases pact.

During this period, the Foreign Minister, Raul Manglapus, launched a new foreign policy initiative, which was seen as an attempt to extricate the Aquino government from an increasingly emotional, domestic debate, by internationalising the issue of the US military presence in the Philippines. During visits to Thailand, Malaysia and Singapore on November 4-7, and Indonesia on November 17, Manglapus proposed that ASEAN countries should accept "shared responsibility" for the bases. He argued that since the bases protected regional security, there should be regional backing for their continued presence. While Thailand was reportedly sympathetic to the idea, sources indicated that both Malaysia and Indonesia rejected it, seeing it, among other things, as a threat to their relations with the non-aligned movement. The matter was raised again at an ASEAN summit meeting in Manila on December 14-16 but no formal position could be agreed. However, the fact that the summit had gone ahead despite security threats was seen as a vote of confidence by ASEAN leaders in President Aquino's government.

Meanwhile, the position of Americans serving in the Philippines appeared increasingly isolated and embattled. On November 18, US servicemen at Subic Bay and Clark Field Air Base were put on the highest state of alert as part of an exercise to prepare against a possible communist assault. It was reported on December 31 that US embassy personnel had had hardship allowances increased because of deteriorating conditions in the country. US business interests were also threatened for the first time, when the NPA announced in early January that US "business empires" in the Philippines were to become "legitimate targets" for attack. A number of US companies had already pulled senior executives out of the country after a warning by the Philippines Chamber of Commerce in early January that they could be attacked.

At the start of 1988, relations between the two countries remained clouded by the political uncertainties in the Philippines. Faced with rising Filipino nationalism, both sides were expected to adopt a cautious approach in the talks on the US bases later in the year. It was reported that both the US government and President Aquino had agreed to limit the scope of the discussions to the question of compensation for the use of the facilities, leaving any broader review of the bases agreement until the climate improved. However, there were fears that even the limited issue of compensation could occasion a contentious public debate which would weaken the already tenuous position of Mrs Aquino still further, as well as affecting the prospects for renewing the base agreement beyond 1991.

ATMOSPHERES AND IMPRESSIONS: GLIMPSES OF THE PHILIPPINES

A load of rubbish on Smoky Mountain

At first sight, it looks like a vast, squat, badly-eroded hill, crouched over the poorer quarters of Navotas, on the northern outskirts of Manila, looming over the dirty waters of Manila Bay. In fact, Smoky Mountain is a load of rubbish; three hundred feet high and several miles square, piled layer upon layer, the result of 30 years of daily dumping. Its lower slopes are sufficiently compacted to support the thousands of cardboard and corrugated iron shacks, permanent home to a scavenging community of some 25,000 people, who earn between 20 and 30 pesos a day collecting scraps of plastic, paper and iron for sale to the recycling plants. Trails of smoke from numerous small fires, caused by the spontaneous combustion of the decaying garbage, merge into an ash-grey fog that clings to the slopes, seeping into the shacks.

All day, every day, the garbage trucks trundle round the mountain's winding roads to the dumping grounds on the summit, where the scavengers, of both sexes and all ages, wait to wade in and sift through the new loads for some choice nugget of plastic or polystyrene. Sometimes fights break out over a particularly valued chunk; sometimes small children, rummaging in the heart of a mound of rubbish, are buried alive in a freshly-tipped load. The uneven, shifting surface of the top layers on the mountain's "summit" claims several victims a year who fall through the thin crust to suffocate to death beneath the garbage. Occasionally their bodies are reared up again by the bulldozers. . .

Smoky Mountain's origins go back to 1954, when this stretch of Manila Bay was filled in as part of a Japanese-financed project to set up new industries on reclaimed land. The scheme failed to attract sufficient investment, however, and soon the idle land was being used as an unofficial rubbish tip. The local fishing community, which had lost its livelihood with the filling of the bay, seized on the opportunity to fend off disaster by selling scrap from the rubbish to local dealers. Some of the original community live there still, but they have since been joined by newcomers from as far away as the southern island of Negros, its economy ravaged by the decline in the sugar industry. To them, the near certainty of 20 pesos a day is salvation compared to the creeping hunger in their homes.

Despite its grim appearance, Smoky Mountain attracts thousands for whom the vast, sprawling metropolis of Manila offers no other hope of work. Two of its inhabitants are Eddie and his wife, Marie, who, together with their two children, live in a hardboard shack, about four metres by three metres square, at the foot of the mountain. Scraps of lino provide the flooring, and the walls are part covered, part held together by fading posters and Pirelli-style commercial calendars. Sanitation is non-existent: "We use the flying saucer method", explains Eddie cheerfully. "We wrap up the waste in newspaper and throw it out the door." Outside, spent "flying saucers" litter the muddy alleys between the huts, a constant source of fascination to the dogs which snuffle around the stagnant puddles.

Unsurprisingly, the mountain has one of the highest child mortality rates in the country. Weakened by diarrhoea, many children are killed off by bronchial pneumonia, TB and other lung diseases, brought on by the acrid, omnipresent fumes. The fact that the mountain lies just a few miles from the sanitized, manicured business and hotel district has guaranteed it sporadic bursts of international media attention, particularly from television crews who are keen to capture its photogenic poverty. Embarrassed by this unwelcome attention, and consequent demands for action, the government periodically undertakes to remove the eyesore and rehouse its occupants. Until now, all such promises have come to nothing, as the authorities seem more concerned with the cosmetics of the operation than with ensuring alternative forms of livelihood for Smoky's residents. In one of her less credible statements, Cory Aquino recently declared the government's intention to demolish the mountain on the grounds that its fumes had become a health hazard to the capital as a whole. The sad irony of her claim lies in the fact that much of Manila is permanently coated in a brown fog of health hazards from the city's unchecked industrial and traffic pollution. Smoky Mountain's contribution is a drop in the ocean.

In one much trumpeted relocation scheme in 1982, hundreds of dwellings on the mountain were demolished, again on "health grounds", and their occupiers transferred to a new project 10km to the south. The government promised jobs and houses, but only came up with a patch of waste ground, divided into small individual "building plots", each with its own latrine—the sole on-site facility. The ex-squatters were expected to build their own shelters, pay for the construction of an access road, and somehow find work in an area where jobs were scarce. Not surprisingly, many chose the devil they knew and made their way home to Smoky Mountain.

REVOLUTION IN THE PHILIPPINES?

Faced with such inertia, the squatters have organized themselves under the banner of the People's Council of the Smoky Mountain. "Banner", incidentally, is no metaphor: inside the Council's school house hangs its flag, an embroidered golden outline of the mountain puffing silver-threaded clouds of smoke on a crimson sky.

Founded in 1983, the People's Council provides rudimentary health care as well as schooling. More ambitiously, it tries to find the key to springing the poverty trap that has made the mountain such a dubious place of refuge. Council members talk eagerly, if vaguely, of the need for vocational training and meaningful relocation schemes to achieve "the social justice which is our right". Suspicious of such politically-tinged rhetoric, the security forces stage sporadic raids on squatter areas like Smoky Mountain in the search for members of the NPA's "sparrow squad" assassination teams. Many of those picked up in such raids are teenagers whose closest involvement with the armed struggle is shooting their mouth off in the wrong company.

Most weekends, the mountain plays host to groups of university students, despatched by their liberal professors to gain some fleeting first-hand experience of poverty. Apparently uninterested in the struggle for survival being waged all around, a small group of impeccably dressed students joked and flirted together outside Eddie and Marie's shack, whiling away the hours until it was time to leave the Third World for their residential compounds up on Manila's airier heights.

MW

A bit of local culture

"Hey Joe!...Hey Man!...Joe, where are you going, what's the problem, Joe?"

To be white in the slums of Manila is to court curiosity from young Filipinos, bemused as to why this "Americano" should have wandered away from the crisply Westernized hotel and business district. The vast majority of visitors to the capital never penetrate beyond this familiar haven of tree-studded boulevards and black glass office blocks—a variation on a theme repeated throughout the developing Asian economies, in Singapore, Taiwan, Seoul... It's as Filipino as Dallas, of course, and its relation to the rest of the city is apparent in the fact that many slum children have never seen a white face except on television—on "Dallas", perhaps.

Western expectations, however, demand that this kit-assembled version of a thrusting new financial centre should reveal some "genuine Filipino culture" by night, in the form of the hostess bars...

ATMOSPHERES AND IMPRESSIONS

"Hey, Joe!—in here—real pretty girls, Joe!". One man bars your way, grinning from ear to ear, his friend throws open the door to allow you a quick glimpse. . . "what's the problem, Joe? You don't like girls? We got some real nice boys, Joe". Inside the clubs, with names like "Blue Lagoon", "Paradise", and, for some dubious but doubtless significant reason, "Shampoo", bleary-eyed businessmen—Americans, Europeans, Japanese, Australian,—lean on the bar, eyeing the dancers with a mixture of embarrassment and cautious interest.

Dressed in surprisingly modest swimsuits, the girls bop away stoically, now and then switching on a practised smile to tease some persistent ogler. With a touch of the absurd, some have enormous plastic combs - an essential accessory for most fashion-conscious young Filipinos - protruding out of their swimsuits. The punters pay a fixed fee to the bar-owner if they want to take a girl back to their hotel. But the notion of some cultural predisposition to easy virtue is well wide of the mark, according to counsellors in a nearby drop-in centre for prostitutes.

"The girls are mostly from village backgrounds, islands like Samar and Leyte, very poor and devout Catholics. They're recruited under false premises; told they'll be working as domestic maids or something similar. But once they've started, it's very difficult for them to leave; the bar's their sole source of income, food and shelter, and besides, they usually manage to send money home, which was the reason for coming to Manila in the first place." Beyond Manila lies the ultimate goal for many of the girls; to get to the West by marrying one of the punters. Once there, so they believe, they'll be able to send enough money home to lift their families out of the rural poverty trap, and maybe even bring them over to their new home. It happens just often enough to keep alive the hopes of the others.

This highly-optimistic hope is enthusiastically fostered by the "mail-order bride" agencies, based in Europe and the USA, which advertize in the personal columns under gushing headings such as "There Is No Greater Love Than A Filipina". Many agencies promise that each bride-to-be comes complete with ideal old-fashioned virtues such as fidelity, obedience and a love of housework, with the added spice of a voracious appetite for sex. Feminism is unknown in the Philippines, claim the agencies, conveniently ignoring women's organizations like GABRIELA, which campaigns against this image under the slogan "A Woman's Place is in the Struggle". A few marriages work; many end in disaster amidst the shattering of expectations on both sides, as the new bride is catapulted into a strange new culture with a husband whom she may have met for a few hours only, at a Manila hotel rendezvous arranged by the agency.

Drag yourself away from the Blue Lagoon, down the street away from the ever-opening doors, and you're back in a world of more familiar soliciting; from a mess of torn clothes in a shop doorway comes the thin voice of an old woman: "Joe. . . Joe, I am hungry".

MW

Bounced through the Cordillera

Dragging itself out of Baguio, the battered, dented, but squeaky clean red bus of the Dangwa-Tranco company heaves its way through the outlying mining communities, as the first daylight picks out the ridge-line high over the winding valley. The bus climbs with the sun, rattling and bouncing over the dirt road which snakes up the slopes of the Cordillera mountains. Its passengers are a mix of urban Filipinos and local Ifugao tribespeople, visiting relatives or returning home after a period of work in the town.

An hour out of Baguio and the landscape is spectacular; waves of mountains, receding into the distance, their slopes sporadically lined with terraces—each step taller than a man, many slopes carrying upwards of 20 steps, sparkling green with the new rice crop. Along the roadside and among the terraces are clusters of Ifugao villages, their huts perched on low stilts. Some retain the traditional thatched roofs, like a squat, pointed hat pulled down over the eyes, others resort to corrugated iron—easier to maintain, but chilly on the cool upland nights.

The bus tumbles and jolts around 180 degree bends, tugging itself precariously round the shoulders of slumped hillsides, sending scatters of roadside pebbles sliding down the scree slopes. At one point, we are stopped short by the debris of some recent minor avalanche; with varying degrees of reluctance, driver and passengers pile out into the fresh highland morning. Muttering curses in a variety of languages, we drag, shove, and, occasionally carry the larger stones to the side of the track. Some slip over the edge, sending new slides skidding down into the pines below. A scruffy wooden sign by the roadside proclaims us to be at the "Highest Point in the Philippines Highway System", before a slow, winding descent along one flank of a long, sinuous valley, now sufficiently wide to allow a continuous string of rice padis along its riverside. As the land falls, the pines give way to coconut palms and bananas; the freshness in the air fades back into tropical heat.

Outside one small town, the bus pulls to a halt at a makeshift roadblock, and several men climb aboard to carry out a cursory search, M-16 rifles slung over their teeshirts and pistols sticking out of their jeans. They peer vaguely along the overhead racks and look at random under a couple of seats, but fail to check the spacious luggage compartment in the side of the bus, big enough to carry arms and ammunition for a small army.

Dismounting, they wave to us shyly as the bus pulls away, then wander back to their companions, one of whom is ostentatiously cleaning his rifle while his friend cracks open the coca-cola. Without uniforms or other evidence, their identity was unclear; probably a local vigilante group, funded by the Army, although later I learned that the NPA had been in the area and staged a public parade in the town. Whoever they were, they weren't looking for trouble.

The road staggers along the valley for another hour's worth of being catapulted from seat into luggage rack, before reaching Bontoc. This old valley town of the eponymous Ifugao tribe is now a single street of nondescript two or three storey buildings. From here, an equally battered Fiera jeep takes over the next stage of the journey; climbing out of the town along a rough track above a valley carpeted with a shiny chequerboard of incandescent rice padis, terraces of them rising up the slopes in intricate, formal but ever-changing beauty. In a tiny village perched on the edge of a stream, the jeep exchanges knots of machete-carrying Ifugaos, unfortunately retaining its cargo of three Australian tourists on the roof, from where, periodically, a jettisoned banana skin plummets down the hillside. Unimpressed by the scenery, they lose themselves in a spirited argument over the relative merits of Lebanese and Thai marijuana.

Through the open doors and windows of the village school, some 40 or so children bend over old-style desks, as if in earnest fulfilment of an order to pose for the passing foreigners. Their teacher, neat and pucker in a starched white dress, completes the pose, pointing at a faded map slung from a blackboard.

Climbing steeply away from the village, the terraces become thinner and more scattered as the trees thicken and diversify; swathes of rainforest that sweep down from the hilltops, giving the impression that it is the trees which are encroaching on the clearings rather than the other way round. Suddenly, on rounding a rocky turn, it stretches out vast and unbroken, across the valley bowl and over the far ridges, dozens of shades of green fading into blue. Like undergrowth run riot and clambering up to a hundred times its normal height, it spreads a tangled mess of giant ferns, some identical to northern bracken but twenty feet high, uncurling fresh fronds almost menacingly, as though pawing at the roadside. The depth and density of the forest is ideal cover for small bands of guerrillas, their recent presence evident in the burnt-out ruins of a solitary military post at the top of a pass, its walls splattered by machine-guns and grenades. Farcically wide of the mark, the Australians knowingly ascribe this to Japanese-American fighting during the last war, despite the fact that the ground around the building is still singed from the fire.

A few miles from Banawe, sporadic clearings reappear, and then a long, looping turn brings us to the "viewpoint"; a cluster of shacks selling tourist trinkets overlook a view of overwhelming beauty: a wide, curving valley meandering hugely into the distance, its slopes covered in perfectly maintained rice terraces, emerald contour lines snaking into the haze, rising in staggered layers, narrowing as they climb the hills, the uppermost slopes of which remain under a protective blanket of rainforest.

Resigned-looking elderly tribespeople hang around in slightly ludicrous "traditional" garb, looking to pick up the odd peso or two from inclusion in a holiday snap. Fortunately, their less anachronistic offspring still manage the terraces, while the lowlanders make a killing from the tourists in Banawe village—a single street given over almost entirely to craft stalls and lodging houses, patronized by travellers from Australia, America and continental Europe. Youth and former youth in shorts and singlets; blonde hair, bronzed bodies and general on-the-road appearance. They join in enthusiastically on the choruses of Beatles and Eagles songs favoured by amateur Filipino guitarists.

It makes a strange tourist centre, isolated on a dirt road surrounded by the looming terraces and forest, in what is effectively a war zone, 200 miles north of Manila. The isolation may soon end; the government has plans to build an asphalt road all the way through to Banawe, not least to ensure improved military access. With some reason, it suspects that many of the highlanders are sympathetic to the NPA. The fragility of the highland landscape is alarmingly apparent up a mere 30 miles to the south; here the forests are felled or reduced to straggling secondary growth; the valleys still rich with rice but the slopes a wizened, dry-brown relic of their former selves, deep gullies of erosion cutting down to the plain, with scarcely a banana bush remaining.

MW

The following three pieces by James Fenton appeared originally in The Independent, to whom the Editor is grateful for permission to reproduce them here. James Fenton has written widely on the Philippines, and currently reports from Manila for The Independent.

When the dead live it up on squid and chocolate biscuits

At this time of the year [early November], the mountain roads near Baguio are strewn with lilies, and the fern-traders of Quezon are doing well. It is the florists' peak season. The price of gladioli and anthuriums goes sky high. All the ethnic Filipinos are buying flowers for their family graves.

Whatever sort of person you are, whatever your temperament, a bit of you feels rotten if you let All Saints' Day or All Souls' Day pass without going to the cemetery, and paying your respects. People travel hundreds of miles to do this, and the buses are packed out well in advance.

You may get an impression of the scale of the festivity from the fact that at La Loma in Manila, the city's north cemetery, people bring ladders to scale its 12-foot walls, to save visitors the time it takes to negotiate the crush at the main gate. You pay a small toll to the owner of the ladder, and a small fee to the man who will guard your parked car. In the street of the cemetery (for it resembles a town) there are sidewalk merchants buying the spilt candle-wax at 30p a kilo. The price of candles is exorbitant, and masses of wax gets spilt.

The Chinese section of the cemetery is the most desirable residential area for the dead: the streets are named, the mausoleums are built of expensive marble and the detail that gives the visitor the creeps is the inclusion of letter-boxes set into the strong steel-and-glass doors. Rumour has it that the Chinese hide their bullion in the family vaults. Certainly at one of the tombs I visited this weekend there was an armed security guard on duty.

A large number of the Chinese are Catholics, but so what. They still believe in giving offerings of food to the dead, whose portraits figure more prominently above the tombs than any of the religious images. And you can see very clearly what sort of food the ancestors valued most highly. They liked Del Monte peach halves. They liked Cadbury's chocolate biscuits, squid and raisin cookies. The key word is "imported"—they liked all the imported fruits. The graves of the wealthy Chinese resemble houses to the extent of having kitchens, comfort rooms and showers. The only thing most of them lack is furniture. But both Chinese and ethnic Filipinos will make themselves at home in the graveyard by bringing televisions, ghetto-blasters, packs of cards, and soft and hard drinks. You keep vigil at the graves, and while you do so it seems only natural to pass the time of night with a disco.

One of the great advantages of All Saints' Day in the provinces is that the young men can get to meet girls. You walk around the cemetery spotting the attractive ones and noting the family names on the tombstone for future reference. The night passes in music, drink and cards. Large quantities of Ginebra San Miguel, the gin known locally by the name "stainless", get consumed, and when people get drunk on stainless they tend to fight.

Tonight, as the festivities draw to a close, a special class of people will be eyeing the Chinese graves, and as soon as the coast is clear they will climb into the area and get the chicken carcasses, the apples and the tin food. If the mausoleums are locked, they will use bamboo rods and hooks and whatever else may be necessary to ease the chocolate biscuits across the polished marble floors to within reach of the windows.

And the ancestors, we may imagine, will watch the tomb-robbers with fastidious unconcern. They will have other things to think about. By now they will know all the family gossip—whether it was in fact a good idea to pull out of real estate and go for sugar futures, whether the eldest son is likely to be a top-notcher in his bar exams, whether a suitable match has been found for that faintly disappointing daughter.

As you read this piece, a tin of peach halves will be edging across a moonlit sarcophagus. The mausoleum shower will be dripping. There will be a heavy smell of joss, wax and stainless. Suddenly, the fridge of the ancestors will turn itself on, the robbers jump and the peaches come crashing to the ground. This is the secret life of the tombs, the latest incidents in their gelid eternity.

JF

How the Dona Paz sank the fishermen's fortunes

I know a man who knows a man who bought a large fish the other day, opened its stomach and found a human ear and a finger. And it occurs to me that if *I* know a man who knows a man to whom this thing happened, then most of Manila must either know a man, or know a man who knows a man, to whom the same thing happened.

The sinking last month [December 1987] of the Dona Paz—in which nobody knows how many people perished because the ship was crammed with passengers not listed on the manifest—was the worst peacetime maritime disaster (if you ignore the fact that the Philippines is not at peace) ever. Some people say the worst "since the Titanic". Since the Titanic nothing. They are only now finding out how many people perished.

On the island of Samar, for instance, 100 primary school teachers failed to turn up at the beginning of term because they are dead. Two hundred pupils were absent for the same reason. Samar is a very poor place. Imagine the difficulties a family from Samar will have proving a relative was on the Dona Paz: more than 3,000 people perished, but only 108 bodies were retrieved.

One presumes the fish have eaten the rest, and even those who have not heard stories about fingers and ears have stopped eating seafood. In my household, freshwater fish began to appear on the table. Anything known to come from a fishpond is OK. But in the markets, an extraordinary drop in the price and sales of fish has been registered.

And this has happened not just in Manila but in Southern Luzon as well. My impression from the Manila markets is that both prices and sales have halved, so that trading is at about 25 per cent of the normal volume.

But this is complicated by the fact that fish prices are high just before Christmas, and normally fall just after.

Also it is complicated by the fact that, if you go to the fish market, some people get angry when referring to the subject. Everyone wants to say their fish do not come from Mindoro, where the accident occurred. But their fish are often labelled as coming from Lucena, very near the scene of the disaster. There is a certain amount of gallows humour among the vendors. But basically, they have been dealt a body-blow.

The psychology seems clear enough: everyone is thinking about what happened to those thousands of missing people. Before I heard the story of my friend's friend finding the ear and the finger, I had thought of the fish boycott as an act of collective mourning for the dead, a kind of protest. The price of meat is stable. Vegetables are going up. People really seem to be expressing a collective opinion of some kind.

And it is not just that they do not want to slit open a large fish and find a finger. They have boycotted crabs that come from the sea, prawns (anyone who has reared prawns will know that they are not too fussy about what they eat), anything that might have benefited from the disaster. When I went to talk to the fishwives, I made a point of buying some seafood, on the straight humanitarian grounds that I do not see why the fishwives should die just because the Dona Paz has been sunk.

After a while, I had bought as much seafood as one household could reasonably be expected to eat. And after I stopped buying, I began to encounter hostility in the interviews. One old woman said her blood pressure was rising just at the thought of the price of fish. I have several friends in the fish trade and do not like to incur such hostility.

But I can also see the point of the fish boycott. So far, it is the only concerted response to the catastrophe. It is an expression of sympathy for the dead. People have accused the government of failing to respond properly. The bereaved have tried to file suits against Sulpicio Lines and to get the firm closed down.

I doubt whether many of them hold much hope of decent compensation. Few people here have a high opinion of Filipino justice. The fish boycott seems like a modest, well-meant, and unconscious memorial for the dead.

JF

Ringing in the new and machine-gunning the past

Theoretically, this business about it being a Chinese custom to make as much noise as possible at the end of the year in order to frighten the evil spirits sounds reasonable enough, until you reflect that (a) it's not the end of the Chinese year, and (b) the vast majority of the Filipinos making all this noise are not Chinese.

Not only are they not Chinese, they detest many things to do with the Chinese. Yet here they are, at the end of—what is it? the Gregorian year? the International Standard year? the un-Chinese year?—anyway, making as much noise as possible.

I doubt if I could describe the noise. It begins days before, and it lasts in a more or less desultory way for a couple of days after. It starts to gain intensity during the afternoon of New Year's Eve. By now, those who have not already bought their fireworks, their toy guns, their paper trumpets and so forth, are beginning to get edgy.

The fireworks themselves are illegal. It is therefore more convenient to buy them outside the city. In fact, as I increasingly find, the best place to get anything done, as long as you want it done in the macho, Filipino bruiser ("cowboy") style, is outside the city. People go to Bulacan, where they purchase their fireworks from the small manufacturers, and reckon to gun-run them past any police they come across on the way home.

And gun-running it is. For the firecrackers, although they come in all sizes, are all to some degree dangerous-sounding, and mostly extremely dangerous. The smallest is the *Watusi*, or Jumping Stick. Next, the *Rebentador*, the *Triangolo*, the *Thunder* and the *Bawang* (or Garlic). *Lolo Thunder* (or Grandfather Thunder) is serious enough to make you wonder, at the distance of 30 ft, whether your hearing has been permanently damaged. Larger than these are the *Baby Dynamite*, the *Whistle Bomb*, and the *Kuwitis* (another of the Spanish-derived names, coming from *cohete*, or rocket).

Finally, there is the *Judas Belt*, which consists usually of 30-odd linked triangles, and which is designed to produce a noise like a brief fire-fight, heard at frighteningly close quarters. Or, if you want, a long fire-fight. When the *Judas Belt* arrived in my house it was the size of a very serious landmine. Unwound, it turned out to be a thousand explosions in length. It was hung in a tree, fuse downwards, and there was much discussion about the timing of its detonation, and whether it might not be *sayang* (a pity) to set it off all at once, and wouldn't it perhaps be better divided into three?

Well, of course, everything about fireworks is *sayang*. That's the essence of them. It's *sayang* to spend all that money on noise. It's *sayang* that the people with access to explosives (which must mean the military here) are selling off their supplies for festive purposes. It's *sayang* that these festivals kill and wound so many people every year. The newspapers all had different figures the next day, but it was clear that around 14 people had been killed and 2,000 wounded.

This is *sayang*. The noise of New Year's Eve is *sayang*. As it grows in intensity, however, the volume of *sayang* is outstripped by the clamour of competition. Everyone becomes alert to the level of his neighbour's consumption of explosives. Towards midnight, the *Judas Belts* are brought out more frequently. Finally, in my neighbourhood, every household really began to show its hand. We had announced earlier, by a series of impressive *Lolo Thunders*, that we had some trump cards to play, but we had resisted the temptation to divide the *Judas Belt*.

And we were quite right, because nobody around us had anything as elaborate as a *Judas Belt* of 1,000 pieces. It definitely made its mark.

You could tell this, because it was only after our *Judas Belt* had gone off that the neighbours began firing their automatic weapons, their revolvers, their machine-pistols, and so on and so forth. We'd smoked them out, and they came out with their guns blazing. None of our neighbours seemed to possess any rogue artillery pieces, we discovered, and this seemed to be comforting. But who knows what sort of *Judas Belt* they, and we, will lay on next year?

JF

Saying yes on the first anniversary of People Power: February 1987

Benigno Aquino assassinated: the "Ninoy" monument

Cutting cane

Jeepneys on the city streets

Finding a living on Smoky Mountain

Cordillera checkpoint

PART THREE: REFERENCE SECTION

ECONOMIC STRUCTURE

AREA, POPULATION AND LANGUAGES

The total land area of the Philippines is 300,810 square km. There are over 7,000 islands, of which the largest are as follows:

Luzon	104,688 square km
Mindanao	94,630 square km
Samar	13,080 square km
Negros	12,705 square km
Palawan	11,785 square km
Panay	11,515 square km
Mindoro	9,735 square km
Leyte	7,214 square km
Cebu	4,422 square km
Bohol	3,865 square km
Masbate	3,269 square km
Others	23,902 square km

The total population in the 1980 census was 48,098,460. In mid-1986, it was officially estimated at 56,004,000. The principal population centres are as follows (figures from 1980 census):

Metro Manila, including Quezon City, Caloocan and Pasay (Luzon)	3,551,936
Davao (Mindanao)	610,375
Cebu (Cebu)	490,281
Zamboanga (Mindanao)	343,722
Bacolod (Negros)	262,415
Iloilo (Panay)	244,827
Cagayan de Oro (Mindanao)	227,312
Angeles (Luzon)	188,834
Butuan (Mindanao)	172,489
Iligan (Mindanao)	167,358
Olongapo (Luzon)	156,430
Batangas (Luzon)	143,570
Cabanatuan (Luzon)	138,298
San Pablo (Luzon)	131,655

The national language is Pilipino, an official form of Tagalog which is spoken widely on Luzon and elsewhere. Of the many other local languages and dialects, the most common are Cebuano, Iloco and Ifugao. English is widely used and understood, particularly in large urban centres, and is to some extent favoured by the ruling élite, either in pure form or in the hybrid "Taglish".

COMMUNICATIONS

There are 161,709 km of public roads in the Philippines, of which approximately half are surfaced. Railways extend to only 1,263 km, the vast majority of which are on Luzon, in the form of two lines extending to the north and south of Manila. A light-rail transit system (Metrorail) was opened in 1984, with two lines serving the Metro Manila area. Further extensions are at the planning stage. The commonest forms of public transport are buses and jeepneys (locally-manufactured motor vehicles, originally based on a design adapted from US Army jeeps, which run fixed routes in all urban areas).

Numerous ferries run between the islands. The coastal shipping fleet in 1980 consisted of 10,500 vessels (including fishing craft). There are two container terminals at Manila, and a further one is planned for Cebu. The Philippines Ports Authority oversees the operation of 94 national ports, 528 municipal ports and 283 privately-operated ports.

Many of the islands have air links; there are 87 public airports and approximately 120 private airfields. International air transport is concentrated on Manila international airport, although there are four alternative international airports at Laoag (northern Luzon); Peurto Princesa (Palawan); and Davao and Zamboanga (Mindanao). The national airline, Philippines Airlines, runs services worldwide. Air traffic is supervized by the Bureau of Air Transportation.

THE MEDIA

Newspapers. There are approximately 35 daily newspapers in the Philippines, of which around 15 are published in Metro Manila. Numerous weeklies and special-interest periodicals are also produced. The principal languages used in the press are English and Tagalog, with Chinese and local languages also represented.

The country's main news agency is the Philippine News Agency (Media Center, Maharlika Broadcasting System, Bohol Avenue, Quezon City, Metro Manila: Telephone 976661; Telex 63465).

Radio and Television. There are about 270 radio stations operating in the Philippines, and five main television networks. The National Telecommunications Commission supervizes all private and public telecommunications.

EMPLOYMENT

The breakdown of employment in the Philippines by sector is as follows (latest available figures are from 1984):

Sector	% Total workforce
Agriculture, forestry and fishing	49.5
Government, community, social and personal services	6.8
Commerce	12.5
Manufacturing	9.9
Transport	4.5
Construction	3.8
Others	3.0

AGRICULTURAL AND INDUSTRIAL PRODUCTION

CROPS

The principal crops grown are as follows (figures show estimated 1985 output in thousands of metric tons):

Sugar cane	16,000
Rice (paddy)	8,300
Coconuts	7,793
Bananas	4,368
Maize	3,542
Vegetables (including melons)	2,199
Cassava (manioc)	2,117
Copra	1,700
Pineapples	1,250
Sweet potatoes	1,005
Mangoes	500

LIVESTOCK

The commonest forms of livestock reared in the Philippines are pigs (estimated 8 million in 1985), buffalo or carabao (4.3 million), goats (1.9 million), cattle (1.9 million) and horses (0.3 million). The Philippines is self-sufficient in pork and poultry, but has to import beef and dairy produce. There is a thriving local fishing industry.

FORESTRY

The estimated total forest reserves of 16,700,000 hectares are being rapidly depleted despite various government conservation initiatives, including a ban on log exports. The principal culprits are illegal logging operations (reported to involve the army in some areas) and incursions by "slash and burn" cultivators, particularly in Mindanao. Reafforestation programmes have failed to have a great impact on the losses; moreover it is not possible to replace the richly diverse dipterocarp rainforest once it has been felled.

MINING

The following metals are mined commercially in the Philippines (1985 production figures given in brackets):

Coal (1,261,600 metric tons)
Salt (421,100 metric tons)
Copper ore (222,200 metric tons)
Chromium ore (111,500 metric tons)
Nickel ore (28,158 metric tons)
Zinc concentrates (1,900 metric tons)
Silver (1,685,400 troy ounces)
Gold (1,063,100 troy ounces)

INDUSTRY

The leading industrial products of the Philippines are listed below:

Raw sugar
Electric energy
Cement
Beer
Cigarettes
Residual fuel oils
Distillate fuel oils
Rubber tyres
Wheat flour
Smelter copper
Vegetable oils
Cotton yarn
Plywood
Chemical wood pulp
Mechanical wood pulp
Woven cotton fabrics
Cotton yarn
Paper and paperboard
Caustic soda
Nitrogenous fertilizers
Phosphate fertilizers

ECONOMIC STRUCTURE

Manufactured gas
Jet fuels
Napthas
Kerosene
Soap
Liquefied petroleum gas
Lubricating oils
Television receivers
Motor cars (assembled)
Lorries and trucks (assembled)
Motorcycles and scooters

TRADE

EXPORTS

Export products	1985 US$ million	1985 % of total	1986 US$ million	1986 % of total
TRADITIONAL EXPORTS	1302	28.1	1275	26.3
of which				
Coconut products	459	9.9	470	9.7
of which				
Coconut oil	347	7.5	333	6.9
Dessicated coconut	76	1.6	44	0.9
Copra meal	36	0.8	75	1.3
Copra——	18	0.4		
Sugar and products	185	4.0	103	2.1
of which				
Centrifugal and refined sugar	169	3.7	87	1.8
Molasses	16	0.3	16	0.3
Forest products	199	4.3	201	4.2
of which				
Logs	39	0.8	27	0.6
Lumber	91	2.0	104	2.1
Plywood	51	1.1	56	1.2
Veneer sheets	12	0.3	9	0.2
Other forestry products	6	0.1	5	0.1
Mineral products	243	5.2	267	5.5
of which				
Copper concentrates	84	1.8	90	1.9
Gold	100	2.2	140	2.9
Chromium ore	12	0.3	11	0.2
Other mineral products	47	1.0	26	0.5
Fruit and vegetables	136	2.9	137	0.7
of which				
Canned pineapple	89	1.9	83	1.7

Pineapple juice	7	0.2	6	0.1
Pineapple concentrates	14	0.3	18	0.4
Other fruits and vegetables	26	0.6	30	0.6
Abaca fibres	17	0.4	13	0.3
Tobacco	25	0.5	21	0.4
Petroleum products	39	0.8	63	1.3
NON-TRADITIONAL EXPORTS	3275	70.8	3447	71.1
of which				
Non-traditional manufactures	2765	59.7	2879	59.5
of which				
Electronics and electrical equipment	1056	22.8	919	19.0
Garments	623	13.5	751	15.6
Textile yarns/fabrics	39	0.8	44	0.9
Footwear	39	0.8	31	0.6
Travel goods and handbags	10	0.2	12	0.2
Wood manufactures	43	0.9	49	1.0
Furniture and fixtures	84	1.8	89	1.8
Chemicals	150	3.2	243	5.0
Copper metal	168	3.6	172	3.6
Non-metallic mineral manufactures	24	0.5	18	0.4
Machinery and transport equipment	30	0.6	45	0.9
Processed foods and beverages	106	2.3	116	2.4
Miscellaneous manufactured articles	136	2.9	159	3.3
Others	257	5.6	231	4.8
Non-traditional commodities	510	11.0	568	11.7
Nickel	64	1.4	15	0.3
Iron ore agglomerates	95	2.1	85	1.8
Bananas	113	2.4	130	2.7
Mangoes	7	0.1	8	0.2
Coffee (raw)	70	1.5	119	2.5
Fish (fresh or simply preserved)	99	2.1	143	3.0
Others	62	1.3	68	1.4
SPECIAL TRANSACTIONS	12	0.3	8	0.2
RE-EXPORTS	40	0.9	112	2.3
TOTAL	4629	100.0	4842	100.0

IMPORTS

	1985		1986	
Import products	US$ million	% of total	US$ million	% of total
CAPITAL GOODS	788	15.4	864	17.1
of which				
Non-electrical machinery	366	7.2	395	7.8
Electrical machinery	293	5.7	333	6.6
Transport equipment	48	0.9	54	1.1
Aircraft, ships and boats	20	0.4	24	0.5
Professional, scientific and instruments	61	1.2	58	1.1

RAW MATERIALS AND INTERMEDIATE GOODS	2198	43.0	2671	53.0
of which				
Wheat	106	2.1	129	2.6
Crude materials (inedible)	150	3.0	229	4.5
of which				
Cotton	25	0.5	33	0.7
Synthetic and artificial fibres	50	1.0	57	1.1
Other inedible crude materials	75	1.5	139	2.8
Animal and vegetable oils and fats	13	0.3	13	0.3
Chemicals	584	11.4	711	14.1
Manufactures	508	10.0	654	13.0
Paper and paper products	65	1.3	73	1.4
Textile yarns, fabrics	140	2.8	207	4.1
Iron and steel	135	2.6	204	4.0
Metal products	75	1.3	58	1.1
Other manufactures	93	1.8	112	2.2
Embroideries	196	3.8	253	5.0
Materials for manufacture of electrical equipment	585	11.4	640	12.7
Iron ore, unagglomerated	56	1.1	42	0.8
MINERAL FUELS AND LUBRICANTS	1452	28.4	869	17.2
CONSUMER GOODS	441	8.6	398	7.9
SPECIAL TRANSACTIONS	232	4.5	242	4.8
TOTAL	5111	100.0	5044	100.0

TRADING PARTNERS

The leading trading partners of the Philippines in 1985 were as follows (percentage of total trading value shown in brackets):

EXPORTS

USA (35.9)
Japan (18.9)
Singapore (5.4)
Hong Kong (4.0)
Malaysia (3.8)
West Germany (3.8)
UK (3.6)
Netherlands (3.1)

IMPORTS

USA (25.1)
Japan (14.0)
Malaysia (7.3)
China (5.4)
Saudi Arabia (5.1)

Kuwait (4.2)
Hong Kong (3.9)
Indonesia (3.5)
Australia (3.4)
Taiwan (3.4)
West Germany (2.8)
Singapore (2.4)

FINANCIAL STRUCTURE

GOVERNMENT ECONOMIC AGENCIES

The Central Bank of the Philippines administers the monetary, banking and credit systems of the Philippines, with the objectives of maintaining internal and external monetary stability, preserving the value and convertibility of the peso and promoting economic conditions conducive to a balanced and sustainable growth of the economy. It is the sole bank of issue and has custody and management of foreign exchange reserves. It oversees the financial and credit system, is a clearing bank and is banker, fiscal agent and financial adviser to the government. It manages the external debt and a number of national and multilateral funds and credit programmes. The capital of the Central Bank is 10,000 million pesos. Following the change of regime in February 1986, the Bank took a number of steps to ease monetary and credit controls, in support of the new government's policies of economic expansion and reduced interest rates. The Bank managed and promoted the Debt to Equity Conversion Programme, by which creditors could transform unpaid debts into equity investment in government-approved projects.

The Development Bank of the Philippines specializes in extending credit for agriculture, small and medium industries, and housing. During the last years of the Marcos regime, the Bank's effectiveness was hampered by an increasing number of non-performing accounts. These liabilities and non-peforming assets were transferred to the government in June 1986, to enable the Bank to renew its lending activities. A revised charter was published in December 1986, reaffirming the Bank's "primary purposes" as the "provision of banking services (for) the medium and long-term needs of agricultural and industrial enterprises, particularly in the countryside, and preferably for small and medium scale enterprises".

The Export Processing Zones Authority (EPZA) seeks to promote designated areas of the Philippines as transit depots for international trading companies, offering various incentives to attract usage of these facilities.

The Human Settlement Development Corporation is concerned with the improvement and development of conditions of life in human settle ments, with particular reference to rural communities in the country's under-developed regions.

The Land Bank provides financial support and services in the context of the government's programmes for agrarian reform and development.

The National Development Company is a state-owned company active in a wide range of commerical enterprises in the industrial and agricultural sectors with the aim of providing a government input into the further economic development of the country, some of its operations being joint ventures with other member countries of the Association of South-East Asian Nations (ASEAN).

The National Economic and Development Authority (NEDA) is the central agency for national development planning and co-ordination of programme implementation. Its purpose is to recommend continuing, co-ordinated and fully integrated social and economic plans and programmes. The NEDA's current activities may be summarized as (i) advising and assisting in formulating economic policy and development plans and programmes (annual and long-range planning); (ii) analysing and initiating government-funded development projects; (iii) co-ordinating foreign economic and technical assistance, maintaining contacts with international financial institutions and assisting public and private bodies in obtaining aid from them; (iv) reviewing ministerial initiatives such as the Tourism Priorities Plan; and (v) co-ordinating statistical activities and preparing the national income accounts.

The National Irrigation Administration, established in 1964, has the task of overseeing the development of the country's irrigation infrastructure, including technical support services to farmers. It operates all national irrigation systems. Current programmes include reforestation work in watershed areas and a number of projects supporting the government's aim of achieving self-sufficency in rice production and of correcting regional imbalances in rice supply and demand.

The Philippine International Trading Corporation (PITC) is a key governmental agency for international marketing operations. It is particularly involved in trading with the communist-bloc countries but also has a substantial presence in Australia, West Germany and the United States, notably through "Philippine international houses" for the promotion of the country's products.

The Private Development Corporation of the Philippines (PDCP) was founded in 1963 as a government-sponsored agency with World Bank financial backing for the purposes of promoting private investment and participation in the country's economy. It is the largest development institution in the Philippines. A Southern Philippines Development Authority (SPDA) exists to promote economic development in the under-developed southern regions.

The Securities and Exchange Commission (SEC) has the exclusive jurisdiction to hear and decide cases involving fraud and misrepresentation committed by directors and officers of corporations. It also has a number of regulatory powers over the registration of corporations and partnerships. Under the Aquino administration, the supervision of the SEC was transferred from the Ministry of Finance to the Office of the President.

STOCK EXCHANGES

There are three stock exchanges in the Philippines: the Makati, Manila and Metropolitan exchanges, all of which are based in the capital. The largest and most influential is the Makati Exchange, which commenced trading operations in 1965. It reached its last trading peak in 1976, and entered into a severe decline in the final period of the Marcos regime before recovering strongly during 1986. In 1987, the Makati Exchange announced plans to increase its membership from the present level of 56, and to allow foreign-based brokers to enter the market.

CHAMBERS OF COMMERCE AND EMPLOYERS' ASSOCIATIONS

The five main chambers of commerce are listed below:

Philippine Chamber of Commerce and Industry

Address. Chamber of Commerce Foundation Building, Magallanes Drive, Intramuros, Metro Manila 2801
Telephone. 481641
Telex. 27181

Chamber of Agriculture and Natural Resources of the Philippines

Address. 5th Floor, Rico House, Amorsolo Street, Legaspi Village, Makati, Metro Manila
Telephone. 856296

Chamber of International Trade

Address. Room 904, L&S Building, No. 1, 1414 Roxas Boulevard, Ermite, Metro Manila

European Chamber of Commerce of the Philippines Inc.

Address. 3rd Floor, Electra House, 115-117 Esteban Street, Legaspi Village, Makati, Metro Manila
Telephone. 854747
Telex. 66045

Federation of Filipino-Chinese Chambers of Commerce and Industry

Address. P.O. Box 23, 6th Floor, Federation Center, Muelle de Binondo Street, Metro Manila
Telephone. 474921.

There are about a dozen major employers' associations, of which the umbrella organization is the Employers Confederation of the Philippines (based at the Chamber of Commerce Foundation Building—see above; telephone 474585; telex 27181).

THE 1987 CONSTITUTION

The principal points of the Constitution, approved in the February 1987 referendum, are summarized below.

Article 1 defines the limits of national territory.

Article 2: Declaration of Principles and State Policies

1. The Philippines is a democratic and republican State. Sovereignty resides in the people and all government authority emanates from them.
2. The Philippines renounces war as an instrument of national policy, adopts the generally accepted principles of international law as part of the law of the land and adheres to the policy of peace, equality, justice, freedom, cooperation, and amity with all nations.
3. Civilian authority is, at all times supreme over the military. The Armed Forces of the Philippines is the protector of the people and the State. Its goal is to secure the sovereignty of the state and the integrity of the national territory.
4. The prime duty of the Government is to serve and protect the people. The Government may call upon the people to defend the State and, in the fulfillment thereof, all citizens may be required, under conditions provided by law, to render personal military, or civil service.
5. The maintenance of peace and order, the protection of life, liberty and property, and the promotion of the general welfare are essential for the enjoyment by all the people of the blessings of democracy.
6. The separation of the Church and State shall be inviolable.
7. The State shall pursue an independent foreign policy. In its relations with other states, the paramount consideration shall be national sovereignty, territorial integrity, national interest, and the right to self-determination.
8. The Philippines, consistent with the national interest, adopts and pursues a policy of freedom from nuclear weapons in its territory.
9. The State shall promote a just and dynamic social order that will ensure the prosperity and independence of the nation and free the people from poverty through policies that provide adequate social services, promote

full employment, a rising standard of living, and an improved quality of life for all.

10. The State shall promote social justice in all phases of national development.

11. The State values the dignity of every human person and guarantees full respect for human rights.

12. The State recognizes the sanctity of family life and shall protect and strengthen the family as a basic autonomous social institution. It shall equally protect the life of the mother and the life of the unborn from conception. The natural and primary right and duty of parents in the rearing of the youth for civic efficiency and the development of moral character shall receive the support of the Government.

13. The State recognizes the vital role of the youth in nation-building and shall promote and protect their physical, moral, spiritual, intellectual, and social well-being. It shall inculcate in the youth patriotism and nationalism, and encourage their involvement in public and civic affairs.

14. The State recognizes the role of women in nation-building and shall ensure the fundamental equality before the law of women and men.

15. The State shall protect and promote the right to health of the people and instill health consciousness among them.

16. The State shall protect and advance the right of the people to a balanced and healthful ecology in accord with the rhythm and harmony of nature.

17. The State shall give priority to education, science and technology, arts, culture and sports to foster patriotism and nationalism, accelerate social progress, and promote total human liberation and development.

18. The State affirms labor as a primary social economic force. It shall protect the rights of workers and promote their welfare.

19. The State shall develop a self-reliant and independent national economy effectively controlled by Filipinos.

20. The State recognizes the indispensable role of the private sector, encourages private enterprise, and provides incentives to needed investments.

21. The State shall promote comprehensive rural development and agrarian reform.

22. The State recognizes and promotes the rights of indigenous cultural communities within the framework of national unity and development.

23. The State shall encourage non-governmental, community-based, or sectoral organizations that promote the welfare of the nation.

24. The State recognizes the vital role of communication and information in nation-building.

25. The State shall ensure the autonomy of local governments.

26. The State shall guarantee equal access to opportunities for public service, and prohibit political dynasties as may be defined by law.

27. The State shall maintain honesty and integrity in the public service and take positive and effective measures against graft and corruption.
28. Subject to reasonable conditions prescribed by law, the State adopts and implements a policy of full public disclosure of all its transactions involving public interest.

Article 3: Bill of Rights

1. No person shall be deprived of life, liberty, or property without due process of law, nor shall any person be denied the equal protection of the laws.
2. The right of the people to be secure in their persons, houses, papers, and effects against unreasonable searches and seizures of whatever nature and for any purpose shall be inviolable, and no search warrant or warrant of arrest shall issue except upon probable cause to be determined personally by the judge after examination under oath or affirmation of the complainant and the witnesses he may produce, and particularly describing the place to be searched and the persons or things to be seized.
3. (1) The privacy of communication and correspondence shall be inviolable except upon lawful order of the court, or when public safety or order requires otherwise as prescribed by law. (2) Any evidence obtained in violation of this or the preceding section shall be inadmissible for any purpose in any proceeding.
4. No law shall be passed abridging the freedom of speech, of expression, or of the press, or the right of the people to peaceably assemble and petition the government for redress of grievances.
5. No law shall be made respecting an establishment of religion, or prohibiting the free exercise thereof. The free exercise and enjoyment of religious profession and worship, without discrimination or preference, shall forever be allowed. No religious tests shall be required for the exercise of civil or political rights.
6. The liberty of abode and of changing the same within the limits prescribed by law shall not be impaired except upon lawful order of the court. Neither shall the right to travel be impaired except in the interest of national security, public safety, or public health, as may be provided by law.
7. The right of the people to information on matters of public concern shall be recognized. Access to official records, and to documents, and papers pertaining to official acts, transactions, or decisions, as well as to government research data used as basis for policy development, shall be afforded the citizen, subject to such limitations as may be provided by law.

8. The right of the people, including those employed in the public and private sectors, to form unions, associations or societies for purposes not contrary to law shall not be abridged.

9. Private property shall not be taken for public use without just compensation.

10. No law impairing the obligation of contracts shall be passed.

11. Free access to the courts and quasi-judicial bodies and adequate legal assistance shall not be denied to any person by reason of poverty.

12. (1) Any person under investigation for the commission of an offense shall have the right to be informed of his right to remain silent and to have competent and independent counsel preferably of his own choice. If the person cannot afford the services of counsel, he must be provided with one. These rights can not be waived except in writing and in the presence of a counsel. (2) No torture, force, violence, threat or intimidation, or any other means which vitiate the free will shall be used against him. Secret detention places, solitary, incommunicado, or other similar forms of detention are prohibited. (3) Any confession or admission obtained in violation of this or the preceding section shall be inadmissible in evidence against him. (4) The law shall provide for penal and civil sanctions for violations of this section as well as compensation to and rehabilitation of victims of torture or similar practices, and their families.

13. All persons, except those charged with offenses punishable by reclusion perpetua when evidence of guilt is strong, shall, before conviction, be bailable by sufficient sureties, or be released on recognizance as may be provided by law. The right to bail shall not be impaired even when the privelege of the writ of habeas corpus is suspended. Excessive bail shall not be required.

14. (1) No person shall be held to answer for a criminal offense without due process of law. (2) In all criminal prosecutions, the accused shall be presumed innocent until the contrary is proved, and shall enjoy the right to be heard by himself and counsel, to be informed of the nature and cause of the accusation against him, to have a speedy, impartial and public trial, to meet the witnesses face to face, and to have compulsory process to secure the attendance of witnesses and the production of evidence in his behalf. However, after arraignment, trial may proceed notwithstanding the absence of the accused provided that he has been duly notified and his failure to appear is unjustifiable.

15. The privelege of the writ of habeas corpus shall not be suspended except in cases of invasion or rebellion when the public safety requires it.

16. All persons shall have the right to a speedy disposition of their cases before all judicial, quasi-judicial, or administrative bodies.

17. No person shall be compelled to be a witness against himself.

18. (1) No person shall be detained solely by reason of his political beliefs and aspirations. (2) No involuntary servitude in any form shall exist

except as a punishment for a crime whereof the party shall have been duly convicted.

19. (1) Excessive fines shall not be imposed, nor cruel, degrading or inhuman punishment inflicted. Neither shall death penalty be imposed, unless, for compelling reasons involving heinous crimes, the Congress hereafter provides for it. Any death penalty already imposed shal be reduced to reclusion perpetua. (2) The employment of physical, psychological or degrading punishment against any prisoner or detainee or the use of substandard or inadequate penal facilities under subhuman conditions shall be dealt with by law.

20. No person shall be imprisoned for debt or non-payment of a poll tax.

21. No person shall be twice put in jeopardy of punishment for the same offense. If an act is punishable by a law and an ordinance, conviction or acquittal under either shall constitute a bar to another prosecution for the same act.

22. No ex post facto law or bill of attainder shall be enacted.

Article 4: Citizenship

1. The following are citizens of the Philippines: (1) Those who are citizens of the Philippines at the time of the adoption of this constitution; (2) Those whose fathers or mothers are citizens of the Philippines; (3) Those born before January 17, 1973, of Filipino mothers, who elect Philippine citizenship upon reaching the age of majority; and (4) Those who are naturalized in accordance with law.

2. Natural-born citizens are those who are citizens of the Philippines from birth without having to perform any act to acquire or perfect their Philippine citizenship in accordance with paragraph (3), Sec. 1 hereof shall be deemed natural-born citizens.

3. Philippine citizenship may be lost or reacquired in the manner provided by law.

4. Citizens of the Philippines who marry aliens shall retain their citizenship, unless by their act or omission they are deemed, under the law, to have renounced it.

5. Dual allegiance of citizens is inimical to the national interest and shall be dealt with by law.

Article 5 confers the right to vote on all Filipino citizens over the age of 18.

Article 6: Legislative Department

1. The legislative power shall be vested in the Congress of the Philippines which shall consist of a Senate and a House of Representatives, except to the extent reserved to the people by the provision on initiative and referendum.

2. The Senate shall be composed of twenty-four Senators who shall be elected at large by the qualified voters of the Philippines, as may be provided by law.

3. No person shall be a Senator unless he is a natural-born citizen of the Philippines, and, on the day of the election, is at least thirty-five years of age, able to read and write, a registered voter, and a resident of the Philippines for not less than two years immediately preceding the day of the election.

4. The term of office of the Senators shall be six years and shall commence, unless otherwise provided by law, at noon on the thirtieth day of June next following their election. No Senator shall serve for more than two consecutive terms. Voluntary renunciation of the office for any length of time shall not be considered as an interruption in the continuity of his service for the full term for which he was elected.

5. (1) The House of Representatives shall be composed of not more than two hundred and fifty members, unless otherwise fixed by law, who shall be elected from legislative districts apportioned among the provinces, cities, and the Metropolitan Manila area in accordance with the number of their respective inhabitants, and on the basis of a uniform and progressive ratio, and those who, as provided by law, shall be elected through a party-list system of registered national, regional, and sectoral parties or organizations. (2) The party-list representatives shall constitute twenty per cent of the total number of representatives including those under the party list. For three consecutive terms after the ratification of this Constitution, one-half of the seats allocated to party-list representatives shall be filled, as provided by law, by selection or election from the labor, peasant, urban poor, indigenous cultural communities, women, youth, and such other sectors as may be provided by law, except the religious sector. (3) Each legislative district shall comprise, as far as practicable, contiguous, compact, and adjacent territory. Each city with a population of at least two hundred and fifty thousand, or each province, shall have at least one representative. (4) Within three years following the return of every census, the Congress shall make a reapportionment of legislative districts based on the standards provided in this section.

6. No person shall be a Member of the House of Representatives unless he is a natural-born citizen of the Philippines and, on the day of the election, is at least twenty-five years of age, able to read and write, and, except the party-list representatives, a registered voter in the district in which he shall be elected, and a resident thereof for a period of not less than one year immediately preceding the day of the election.

7. The Members of the House of Representatives shall be elected for a term of three years which shall begin, unless otherwise provided by law, at noon on the thirtieth day of June next following their election. No

Member of the House of Representatives shall serve for more than three consecutive terms. Voluntary renunciation of the office for any length of time shall not be considered as an interruption in the continuity of his service for the full term for which he was elected.

8. Unless otherwise provided by law, the regular election of the Senators and the Members of the House of Representatives shall be held on the second Monday of May.

The remainder of the article provides for the proper conduct of congressmen and for the establishment of Electoral Tribunals and, in the case of the Senate, a Commission of Appointments. It also covers the approval of finance bills and the presidential veto (which may be overriden by a of two-thirds majority of both houses).

Article 7: Executive Department. This article provides for the posts of President and Vice-President. Section 2 specifies:

No person may be elected President unless he is a natural-born citizen of the Philippines, a registered voter, able to read and write, at least forty years of age on the day of the election, and a resident of the Philippines for at least ten years immediately preceding such election.

The same terms apply to the Vice-President. The President's tenure is limited to a single term of six years, while the Vice-President can serve two such terms. Sections 3-6 provide for the election procedure. Sections 7-12 cover the questions of succession and resignation as follows:

7. The President-elect and the Vice-President-elect shall assume office at the beginning of their terms. If the President-elect fails to qualify, the Vice-President-elect shall act as President until the President-elect shall have qualified. If a President shall not have been chosen, the Vice-President-elect shall act as President until a President shall have been chosen and qualified. If at the beginning of the term of the President, the President-elect shall have died or shall have become permanently disabled, the Vice-President-elect shall become President. Where no President and Vice-President shall have been chosen or shall have qualified, or where both shall have died or become permanently disabled, the president of the Senate or, in case of his inability, the Speaker of the House of Representatives shall act as President until a President or a Vice-President shall have been chosen and qualified. The Congress shall, by law, provide for the manner in which one who is to act as president shall be selected until a President or a Vice-President shall have qualified, in case of death, permanent diability, or inability of the officials mentioned in the next preceding paragraph.

8. In case of death, permanent disability, removal from office, or resignation of the President, the Vice-President shall become the President to serve the unexpired term. In case of death, permanent disability, removal from office, or resignation of both the President and Vice-President, the President of the Senate or, in case of his inability, the

Speaker of the House of Representatives, shall then act as President until the President or Vice-President shall have been elected and qualified. The Congress, shall, by law, provide who shall serve as President in case of death, permanent disability, or resignation of the Acting President. He shall serve until the President or the Vice-President shall have been elected and qualified, and be subject to the same restrictions of powers and disqualifications as the Acting President.

9. Whenever there is a vacancy in the Office of the Vice-President during the term for which he was elected, the President shall nominate a Vice-President from among the Members of the Senate and the House of Representaives who shall assume office upon confirmation by a majority vote of all the Members of both Houses of the Congress, voting separately.

10. The Congress, shall, at ten o'clock in the morning of the third day after the vacancy occurs, convene in accordance with its rules without need of a call and within seven days enact a law calling for a special election to elect a President and a Vice-President to be held not earlier than forty-five days nor later than sixty days from the time of such call. The bill calling such special election shall be deemed certified under paragraph 2, Section 26, Article VI of this Constitution and shall become law upon its approval on third reading by the Congress. Appropriations for the special election shall be charged against any current appropriations and shall be exempt from the requirements of paragraph 4, Section 25, Article VI of this Constitution. The convening of the Congress cannot be suspended nor the special election postponed. No special election shall be called if the vacancy occurs within eighteen months before the date of the next presidential election.

11. Whenever the President transmits to the President of the Senate and the Speaker of the House of Representaties his written declaration that he is unable to discharge the powers and duties of his office, and until he transmits to them a written declaration to the contrary, such powers and duties shall be discharged by the Vice-President as Acting President. Whenever a majority of all the Members of the Cabinet transmit to the President of the Senate and to the Speaker of the House of Representatives their written declaration that the President is unable to discharge the powers and duties of his office, the Vice-president shall immediately assume the powers and duties of the office as Acting President. Thereafter, when the President transmits to the President of the Senate and to the Speaker of the House of Rpresentatives his written declaration that no inability exists, he shall reassume the powers and duties of his office. Meanwhile, should a majority of all the Members of the Cabinet transmit within five days to the President of the Senate and to the Speaker of the House of Representatives their written declaration that the President is unable to discharge the powers and duties of his

office, the Congress shall decide the issue. For that purpose, the Congress shall convene, if it is not in session, within forty-eight hours, in accordance with its rules and without need of call. If the Congress, within ten days after receipt of the last written declaration, or, if not in session, within twelve days after it is required to assemble, determines by a two-thirds vote of both Houses, voting separately, that the President is unable to discharge the powers and duties of his office, the Vice-President shall act as President; otherwise, the President shall continue exercising the powers and duties of his office.

12. In case of serious illness of the President, the public shall be informed of the state of his health. The Members of the Cabinet in charge of national security and foreign relations and the Chief of Staff of the Armed Forces of the Philippines, shall not be denied access to the President during such illness.

Sections 13-17 cover presidential appointments.

13. The President, Vice-President, the Members of the Cabinet, and their deputies or assistants shall not, unless otherwise provided in this Constitution, hold any other office or employment during their tenure. They shall not, during said tenure, directly or indirectly, practice any other profession, participate in any business, or be financially interested in any contract with, or in any franchise, or special privilege granted by the Government or any subdivision, agency, or instrumentality thereof, including government-owned or controlled corporations or their subsidiaries. They shall strictly avoid conflict of interest in the conduct of their office. The spouse and relatives by consanguinity or affinity within the fourth civil degree of the President shall not during his tenure be appointed as Members of the Constitutional Commissions, or the Office of the Ombudsman, or as Secretaries, Undersecretaries, chairmen or heads of bureaus or offices, including government-owned or controlled corporations and their subsidiaries.

14. Appointments extended by an Acting President shall remain effective, unless revoked by the elected President within ninety days from his assumption or reassumption of office.

15. Two months immediately before the next presidential elections and up to the end of his term, a President or Acting President shall not make appointments, except temporary appointments to executive positions when continued vacancies therein will prejudice public service or endanger public safety.

16. The President shall nominate and, with the consent of the Commission on Appointments, appoint the heads of the executive departments, ambassadors, other public ministers and consuls, or officers of the armed forces from the rank of colonel or naval captain, and other officers whose appointments are vested in him in this Constitution. He

shall also appoint all other officers of the government whose appointments are not otherwise provided for by law, and those whom he may be authorized by law to appoint. The Congress may, by law, vest the appointment of other officers lower in rank in the President alone, in the courts, or in the heads of departments, agencies, commissions, or boards. The President shall have the power to make appointments during the recess of the Congress, whether voluntary or compulsory, but such appointments shall be effective only until disapproval by the Commission on Appointments or until the next adjournment of the Congress.

17. The President shall have control of all the executive departments, bureaus, and offices. He shall ensure that the laws be faithfully executed. Section 18 deals with emergency powers and martial law.

18. The President shall be the Commander-in-Chief of all armed forces of the Philippines and whenever it becomes necessary, he may call out such armed forces to prevent or suppress lawless violence, invasion or rebellion. In case of invasion or rebellion, when the public safety requires it, he may, for a period not exceeding sixty days, suspend the privilege of the writ of habeas corpus or place the Philippines or any part thereof under martial law. Within forty-eight hours from the proclamation of martial law or the suspension of the privilege of the writ of habeas corpus, the president shall submit a report in person or in writing to the Congress. The Congress, voting jointly, by a vote of at least a majority of all its Members in regular or special session, may revoke such proclamation or suspension, which revocation shall not be set aside by the President. Upon the initiative of the President, the Congress may, in the same manner, extend such proclamation or suspension for a period to be determined by the Congress, if the invasion or rebellion shall persist and public safety requires it. The Congress, if not in session, shall, within twenty-four hours following such proclamation or suspension, convene in accordance with its rules without need of a call. The Supreme Court may review, in an appropriate proceeding filed by any citizen, the sufficiency of the factual basis of the proclamation of martial law or the suspension of the privilege of the writ or the extension thereof, and must promulgate its decision thereon within thirty days from its filing. A state of martial law does not suspend the operation of the Constitution, nor supplant the functioning of the civil courts or legislative assemblies, nor authorize the conferment of jurisdiction on military courts and agencies over civilians where civil courts are able to function, nor automatically suspend the privilege of the writ. The suspension of the privilege of the writ shall apply only to persons judicially charged for rebellion or offenses inherent in or directly connected with invasion. During the suspension of the privilege of the writ, any person thus arrested or detained shall be judicially charged within three days, otherwise he shall be released.

Article 8 covers the judicial department and includes regulations governing the Supreme Court:

4. (1) The Supreme Court shall be composed of a Chief Justice and fourteen Associate Justices. It may sit en banc or, in its discretion, in divisions of three, five, or seven Members. Any vacancy shall be filled within ninety days from the occurrence thereof. (2) All cases involving the constitutionality of a treaty international or executive agreement, or law, which shall be heard by the Supreme Court en banc, including those involving the constitutionality, application, or operation of presidential decrees, proclamations, orders, instructions, ordinances, and other regulations, shall be decided with the concurrence of a majority of the Members who actually took part in the deliberations on the issues in the case and voted thereon. (3) Cases or matters heard by a division shall be decided or resolved with the concurrence of a majority of the Members who actually took part in the deliberations on the issues in the case and voted thereon, and in no case, without the concurrence of at least three of such Members. When the required number is not obtained, the case shall be decided en banc; Provided, that no doctrine or principle of law laid down by the court in a decision rendered en banc or in division may be modified or reversed except by the court sitting en banc:

5. The Supreme Court shall have the following powers: (1) Exercise original jurisdiction over cases affecting ambassadors, other public ministers and consuls, and over petitions for certiorari, prohibition, mandamus, quo warranto, and habeas corpus. (2) Review, revise, reverse, modify, or affirm on appeal or certiorari, as the law or the Rules of Court may provide, final judgments and orders of lower courts in: (a) All cases in which the constitutionality or validity of any treaty, international or executive agreement, law, presidential decree, proclamation, order, instruction, ordinance, or regulation is in question. (b) All cases involving the legality of any tax, impost, assessment, or toll, or any penalty imposed in relation thereto. (c) All cases in which the jurisdiction of any lower court is issue. (d) All criminal cases in which the penalty imposed is reclusión perpetua or higher. (e) All cases in which only an error or question of law is involved. (3) Assign temporarily judges of lower courts to other stations as public interest may require. Such temporary assignment shall not exceed six months without the consent of the judge concerned. (4) Order a change of venue or place of trial to avoid a miscarriage of justice. (5) Promulgate rules concerning the protection and enforcement of constitutional rights, pleading, practice, and procedure in all courts, the admission to the practice of law, the Integrated Bar, and legal assistance to the underprivileged. Such rules shall provide a simplified and inexpensive procedure for the speedy disposition of cases, shall be uniform for all courts of the same grade, and shall not diminish, increase, or modify substantive rights. Rules of procedure of special courts and quasi-judicial bodies shall remain effective unless disapproved

by the Supreme Court. (6) Appoint all officials and employees of the Judiciary in accordance with the Civil Service Law.

6. The Supreme Court shall have administrative supervision over all courts and the personnel thereof.

7. (1) No person shall be appointed Member of the Supreme Court or any lower collegiate court unless he is a natural-born citizen of the Philippines. A Member of the Supreme Court must be at least forty years of age, and must have been for fifteen years or more a judge of a lower court or engaged in the practice of law in the Philippines. (2) The Congress shall prescribe the qualifications of judges of lower courts, but no person may be appointed judge thereof unless he is a citizen of the Philippines and a member of the Philippine Bar. (3) A Member of the Judiciary must be a person of proven competence, integrity, probity, and independence.

Article 9 provides for the establishment of four *"constitutional commissions"*: The Civil Service Commission, the Commission on Elections and the Commission on Audit. Their roles are defined as follows:

The Civil Service Commission, as the central personnel agency of the Government, shall establish a career service and adopt measures to promote morale, efficiency, integrity, responsiveness, progressiveness, and courtesy in the civil service. It shall strengthen the merit and rewards system, integrate all human resources development programs for all levels and ranks, and institutionalize a management climate conducive to public accountability. It shall submit to the President and the Congress an annual report on its personnel programs.

The Commission on Elections is responsible for the conduct of free and fair elections with the following powers: (1) Enforce and administer all laws and regulations relative to the conduct of an election, plebiscite, initiative, referendum, and recall. (2) Exercise exclusive original jurisdiction over all contests relating to the elections, returns, and qualifications of all elective regional, provincial, and city officials, and appellate jurisdiction over all contests involving elective municipal officials decided by trial courts of general jurisdiction, or involving elective barangay officials decided by trial courts of limited jurisdiction. Decisions, final orders, or rulings of the Commission on election contests involving elective municipal and barangay offices shall be final, executory, and not appealable. (3) Decide, except those involving the right to vote, all questions affecting elections, including determination of the number and location of polling places, appointment of election officials and inspectors, and registration of voters. (4) Deputize, with the concurrence of the President, law enforcement agencies and instrumentalities of the Government, including the Armed Forces of the Philippines, for the exclusive purpose of ensuring free, orderly, honest, peaceful, and credible elections. (5) Register, after sufficient publication, political parties, organizations, or coalitions which, in addition to other requirements, must present their platform or program of government; and accredit citizens' arms of the Commission on Elections. Religious denominations and sects shall not be registered. Those which seek to achieve their goals through violence or unlawful means, or refuse to uphold and adhere to this Constitution, or which are supported by any foreign government shall likewise be refused registration. Financial contributions from foreign governments and their agencies to political parties, organizations, coalitions, or candidates related to elections constitute interference in national affairs, and, when accepted, shall be an additional ground for the cancellation of their registration with the Commission, in addition to other penalties that may be prescribed by law. (6) File, upon a verified complaint, or on its own initiative, petitions in court for inclusion or exclusion of voters; investigate and, where appropriate, prosecute cases of violations of election laws, including acts or omissions constituting election frauds, offenses, and malpractices. (7) Recommend to the Congress effective measures to minimize election spending, including limitation of places where propaganda materials shall be posted, and to prevent and penalize all forms of election frauds, offenses, malpractices, and nuisance candidacies. (8) Recommend to the President the removal of any officer or employee it has deputized, or the imposition of any other disciplinary action, for violation or disregard of, or disobedience to its directive, order, or decision. (9) Submit to the President and the Congress a comprehensive report on the conduct of each election, plebiscite, initiative, referendum, or recall.

The Commission on Audit shall have the power, authority, and duty to examine, audit, and settle all accounts pertaining to the revenue and receipts of, and expenditures or uses of funds and property, owned or held in trust by, or pertaining to, the Government, or any of its subdivisions, agencies, or instrumentalities, including government-owned and controlled corporations with original charters, and on a post-audit basis: (a) constitutional bodies, commissions and offices that have been granted fiscal autonomy under this Constitution; (b) autonomous state colleges and universities; (c) other government-owned or controlled corporations with original charters and their subsidiaries; and (d) such non-governmental entities receiving subsidy or equity, directly or indirectly, from or through the Government, which are required by law of the granting institution to submit to such audit as a condition of subsidy or equity. However, where the internal control system of the audited agencies is inadequate, the Commission may adopt such measures, including temporary or special pre-audit, as are necessary and appropriate to correct the deficiencies. It shall keep the general accounts of the government and, for such period as may be provided by law, preserve the vouchers and other supporting papers pertaining thereto. The Commission shall have exclusive authority, subject to the limitations in this Article, to define the scope of its audit and examination, establish the techniques and methods required therefor, and promulgate accounting and auditing rules and regulations, including those for the prevention and disallowance of irregular, unnecessary, excessive, extravagant, or unconscionable expenditures, or uses of government funds and properties.

Article 10 deals with *local government*, providing for the collection of local taxes and the election of officials, their terms to be limited to three years. Section 15-21 cover the provisions for the autonomous regions in Mindanao and the Cordillera.

15. There shall be created autonomous regions in Muslim Mindanao and in the Cordilleras consisting of provinces, cities, municipalities, and geographical areas sharing common and distinctive historical and cultural heritage, economic and social structures, and other relevant characteristics within the framework of this Constitution and the national sovereignty as well as territorial integrity of the Republic of the Philippines.

16. The President shall exercise general supervision over autonomous regions to ensure that laws are faithfully executed.

17. All powers, functions, and responsibilities not granted by this Constitution or by law to the autonomous regions shall be vested in the National Government.

18. The Congress shall enact an organic act for each autonomous region with the assistance and participation of the regional consultative commission composed of representatives appointed by the President from a list of nominees from multisectoral bodies. The organic act shall define the basic structure of government for the region consisting of the executive department and legislative assembly, both of which shall be elective and representative of the constituent political units. The organic acts shall likewise provide for special courts with personal, family, and property law jurisdiction consistent with the provisions of this Constitution and national laws. The creation of the autonomous region shall be effective when approved by majority of the votes cast by the constituent units in a plebiscite called for the purpose, provided that only provinces, cities, and geographic areas voting favorably in such plebiscite shall be included in the autonomous region.

19. The first Congress elected under this Constitution shall, within eighteen months from the time of organization of both Houses, pass the organic acts for the autonomous regions in Muslim Mindanao and the Cordilleras.

20. Within its territorial jurisdiction and subject to the provisions of this Constitution and national laws, the organic act of autonomous regions

shall provide for legislative powers over: (1) Administrative organization; (2) Creation of sources of revenues; (3) Ancestral domain and natural resources; (4) Personal, family, and property relations; (5) Regional urban and rural planning development; (6) Economic, social, and tourism development; (7) Educational policies; (8) Preservation and development of the cultural heritage; and (9) Such other matters as may be authorized by law for the promotion of the general welfare of the people of the region.

21. The preservation of peace and order within the regions shall be the responsibility of the local police agencies which shall be organized, maintained, supervised, and utilized in accordance with applicable laws. The defense and security of the regions shall be the responsibility of the National Government.

Article 11 covers *public accountability*, and allows Congress to initiate and decide cases of impeachment against the President, Vice-President, members of the Supreme Court, constitutional commissions and the Ombudsman (a post created by this Article). In each case, the initiation of impeachment must be by the House of Representatives, with the Senate having sole authority to try and decide each case.

Article 12: National Economy and Patrimony.

1. The goals of the national economy are a more equitable distribution of opportunities, income, and wealth; a sustained increase in the amount of goods and services produced by the nation for the benefit of the people; and an expanding productivity as the key to raising the quality of life for all, especially the underprivileged. The State shall promote industrialization and full employment based on sound agricultural development and agrarian reform, through industries that make full and efficient use of human and natural resources, and which are competitive in both domestic and foreign markets. However, the State shall protect Filipino enterprises against unfair foreign competition and trade practices. In the pursuit of these goals, all sectors of the economy and all regions of the country shall be given optimum opportunity to develop. Private enterprises, including corporations, cooperatives, and similar collective organizations, shall be encouraged to broaden the base of their ownership.

2. All lands of the public domain, waters, minerals, coal, petroleum, and other mineral oils, all forces of potential energy, fisheries, forests or timber, wildlife, flora and fauna, and other natural resources are owned by the State. With the exception of agricultural lands, all other natural resources shall not be alienated. The exploration, development, and utilization of natural resources shall be under the full control and

supervision of the State. The State may directly undertake such activities, or it may enter into co-production, joint venture, or production-sharing agreements with Filipino citizens, or corporations or associations at least sixty per centum of whose capital is owned by such citizens. Such agreements may be for a period not exceeding twenty-five years, renewable for not more than twenty-five years, and under such terms and conditions as may be provided by law. In cases of water rights for irrigation, water supply, fisheries, or industrial uses other than the development of water power, beneficial use may be the measure and limit of the grant. The State shall protect the nation's marine wealth in its archipelagic waters, territorial sea, and exclusive economic zone, and reserve its use and enjoyment exclusively to Filipino citizens. The Congress may, by law, allow small-scale utilization of natural resources by Filipino citizens, as well as cooperative fish farming, with priority to subsistence fishermen and fishworkers in rivers, lakes, bays, and lagoons. The President may enter into agreements with foreign-owned corporations involving either technical or financial assistance for large-scale exploration, development, and utilization of minerals, petroleum, and other mineral oils according to the general terms and conditions provided by law, based on real contributions to the economic growth and general welfare of the country. In such agreements, the State shall promote the development and use of local scientific and technical resources. The President shall notify the Congress of every contract entered into in accordance with this provision, within thirty days from its execution.

3. Lands of the public domain are classified into agricultural, forest or timber, mineral lands, and national parks. Agricultural lands of the public domain may be further classified by law according to the uses to which they may be devoted. Alienable lands of the public domain shall be limited to agricultural lands. Private corporations or associations may not hold such alienable lands of the public domain except by lease, for a period not exceeding twenty-five years, renewable for not more than twenty-five years, and not to exceed one thousand hectares in area. Citizens of the Philippines may lease not more than five hundred hectares, or acquire not more than twelve hectares thereof by purchase, homestead, or grant. Taking into account the requirements of conservation, ecology and development, and subject to the requirements of agrarian reform, the Congress shall determine, by law, the size of lands of the public domain which may be acquired, developed, held, or leased and the conditions therefor.

4. Congress shall, as soon as possible, determine by law the specific limits of forest lands and national parks, marking clearly their boundaries on the ground. Thereafter, such forest lands and national parks shall be conserved and may not be increased nor diminished, except by law. The

Congress shall provide, for such period as it may determine, measures to prohibit logging in endangered forests and watershed areas.

5. The State, subject to the provisions of this Constitution and national development policies and programs, shall protect the rights of indigenous cultural communities to their ancestral lands to ensure their economic, social, and cultural well-being. The Congress may provide for the applicability of customary laws governing property rights or relations in determining the ownership and extent of ancestral domain.

The remaining sections cover points of general economic policy.

Article 13: Social Justice and Human Rights

1. The Congress shall give highest priority to the enactment of measures that protect and enhance the right of all the people to human dignity, reduce social, economic, and political inequalities, and remove cultural inequities by equitably diffusing wealth and political power for the common good. To this end, the State shall regulate the acquisition, ownership, use, and disposition of property and its increments.

2. The promotion of social justice shall include the commitment to create economic opportunities based on freedom of initiative and self-reliance.

3. The State shall afford full protection to labor, local and overseas, organized and unorganized, and promote full employment and equality of employment opportunities for all. It shall guarantee the rights of all workers to self-organization, collective bargaining and negotiations, and peaceful concerted activities including the right to strike in accordance with law. They shall be entitled to security of tenure, humane conditions of work, and a living wage. They shall also participate in policy and decision-making processes affecting their rights and benefits as may be provided by law. The State shall promote the principle of shared responsibility between workers and employers and the preferential use of voluntary modes in settling disputes, including conciliation, and shall enforce their mutual compliance therewith to foster industrial peace. The State shall regulate the relations between workers and employers recognizing the right of labor to its share in the fruits of production and the right of enterprises to reasonable returns on investments, and to expansion and growth.

4. The State shall, by law, undertake an agrarian reform program founded on the right of farmers and regular farmworkers, who are landless, to own directly or collectively the lands they till or, in the case of other farmworkers, to receive a just share of the fruits thereof. To this end, the State shall encourage and undertake the just distribution of all agricultural lands, subject to such priorities and reasonable retention limits, the State shall respect the rights of small landowners. The State shall further provide incentives for voluntary land-sharing.

5. The State shall recognize the right of farmers, farmworkers, and landowners, as well as cooperatives, and other independent farmers' organizations to participate in the planning, organization, and management of the program, and shall provide support to agriculture through appropriate technology and research, and adequate financial, production, marketing, and other support services.

6. The State shall apply the principles of agrarian reform or stewardship, whenever applicable in accordane with law, in the disposition or utilization of other natural resources, including lands of the public domain under lease or concession suitable to agriculture, subject to prior rights, homestead rights of small settlers, and the rights of indigenous communities to their ancestral lands. The State may resettle landless farmers and farmworkers in its own agricultural estates which shall be distributed to them in the manner provided by law.

7. The State shall protect the rights of subsistence fishermen, especially of local communities, to the preferential use of the communal marine and fishing resources, both inland and offshore. It shall provide support to such fishermen through appropriate technology and research, adequate financial, production, and marketing assistance, and other services. The State shall also protect, develop, and conserve such resources. The protection shall extend to offshore fishing grounds of subsistence fishermen against foreign intrusion. Fishworkers shall receive a just share from their labor in the utilization of marine and fishing resources.

8. The State shall provide incentives to landowners to invest the proceeds of the agrarian reform program to promote industrialization, employment creation, and privatization of public sector enterprises. Financial instruments used as payment for their lands shall be honored as equity in enterprises of their choice.

9. The State shall, by law, and for the common good, undertake, in cooperation with the private sector, a continuing program of urban land reform and housing which will make available at affordable cost decent housing and basic services to underprivileged and homeless citizens in urban centers and resettlement areas. It shall also promote adequate employment opportunities to such citizens. In the implementation of such program the State shall respect the rights of small property owners.

10. Urban or rural poor dwellers shall not be evicted nor their dwellings demolished, except in accordance with law and in a just and humane manner. No resettlement of urban or rural dwellers shall be undertaken without adequate consultation with them and the communities where they are to be relocated.

11. The State shall adopt an integrated and comprehensive approach to health development which shall endeavor to make essential goods, health and other social services available to all the people at affordable cost. There shall be priority for the needs of the underprivileged sick, elderly,

disabled, women, and children. The State shall endeavor to provide free medical care to paupers.

12. The State shall establish and maintain an effective food and drug regulatory system and undertake appropriate health manpower development and research, responsive to the country's health needs and problems.

13. The State shall establish a special agency for disabled persons for their rehabilitation, self-development and self-reliance, and their integration into the mainstream of society.

14. The State shall protect working women by providing safe and healthful working conditions, taking into account their maternal functions, and such facilities and opportunities that will enhance their welfare and enable them to realize their full potential in the service of the nation.

15. The State shall respect the role of independent people's organizations to enable the people to pursue and protect, within the democratic framework, their legitimate and collective interests and aspirations through peaceful and lawful means. People's organizations are bona fide associations of citizens with demonstrated capacity to promote the public interest and with identifiable leadership, membership, and structure.

16. The right of the people and their organizations to effective and reasonable participation at all levels of social, political and economic decision-making shall not be abridged. The State shall, by law, facilitate the establishment of adequate consultation mechanisms.

17. (1) There is hereby created an independent office called Commission on Human Rights. (2) The Commission shall be composed of a Chairman and four Members who must be natural-born citizens of the Philippines and a majority of whom shall be members of the Bar. The term of office and other qualifications and disabilities of the Members of the Commission shall be provided by law. (3) Until this Commission is constituted, the existing Presidential Committee on Human Rights shall continue to exercise its present functions and powers. (4) The approved annual appropriations of the Commission shall be automatically and regularly released.

18. The Commission on Human Rights shall have the following powers and functions: (1) Investigate, on its own or on complaint by any party, all forms of human rights violations involving civil and political rights; (2) Adopt its operational guidelines and rules of procedure, and cite for contempt for violations thereof in accordance with the Rules of Court; (3) Provide appropriate legal measures for the protection of human rights of all persons within the Philippines, as well as Filipinos residing abroad, and provide for preventive measures and legal aid services to the underprivileged whose human rights have been violated or need protection; (4) Exercise visitatorial powers over jails, prisons, or

detention facilities; (5) Establish a continuing program of research, education, and information to enhance respect for the primacy of human rights; (6) Recommend to the Congress effective measures to promote human rights and to provide for compensation to victims of violations of human rights, or their families. (7) Monitor the Philippine Government's compliance with international treaty obligations on human rights; (8) Grant immunity from prosecution to any person whose testimony or whose possession of documents or other evidence is necessary or convenient to determine the truth in any investigation conducted by it or under its authority; (9) Request the assistance of any department, bureau, office, or agency in the performance of its functions; (10) Appoint its officers and employees in accordance with law; and (11) Perform such other duties and functions as may be provided by law.

19. The Congress may provide for other cases of violations of human rights that should fall within the authority of the Commission, taking into account its recommendations.

Article 14: Education, Science and Technology, Arts, Culture and Sports. This article outlines the State's responsibilities to encourage achievment in these fields, notably through the maintenance of a national education system. The Article also dealt with the question of official languages: The national language of the Philippines is Filipino. As it evolves, it shall be further developed and enriched on the basis of existing Philippine and other languages. Subject to provisions of law as the Congress may deem appropriate, the Government shall take steps to initiate and sustain the use of Filipino as a medium of official communication and as language of instruction in the educational system. For purposes of communication and instruction, the official languages of the Philippines are Filipino and, until otherwise provided by law, English. The regional languages are the auxiliary official languages in the regions and shall serve as auxiliary media of instruction therein. Spanish and Arabic shall be promoted on a voluntary and optional basis.

Article 15 outlined the State's commitment to the principle of *The Family* as "the foundation of the nation".

Article 16: General Provisions, Section 5 covered the various points relating to the armed forced as follows: (1) All members of the armed forces shall take an oath or affirmation to uphold and defend this Constitution. (2) The State shall strengthen the patriotic spirit and nationalist consciousness of the military, and respect for people's rights in the performance of their duty. (3) Professionalism in the armed forced and adequate remuneration and benefits of its members shall be a prime concern of the State. The armed forces shall be insulated from partisan politics. No member of the military shall engage directly or indirectly in any partisan political activity, except to vote. (4) No member of the armed forces in the active service shall, at any time, be appointed or designated in any capacity to a civilian position in the Government including government-owned or controlled corporations or any of their subsidiaries. (5) Laws on retirement of military officers shall not allow extension of their service. (6) The officers and men of the regular force of the armed forces shall be recruited proportionately from all provinces and cities as far as practicable. (7) The tour of duty of the Chief of Staff of the armed forces shall not exceed three years. However, in times of war or other national emergency declared by the Congress, the President may extend such tour of duty.

Section 11 specified: The ownership and management of mass media shall be limited to citizens of the Philippines, or to corporations, cooperatives or associations, wholly-owned and managed by such citizens. The Congress shall regulate or prohibit monopolies in commercial mass media when the public interest so requires. No combinations in restraint of trade or unfair competition therein shall be allowed.

Article 17 provided the framework under which the Constitution could be amended, either by a three-quarters majority vote of Congress or by a "constitutional convention", to be called either by a two-thirds majority of Congress, or by a public referendum sanctioned by a simple congressional majority. An amendment could also be initiated by a public petition, signed by 12 per cent of registered voters, and approved by a simple majority in a referendum.

Article 18 covered*"Transitory Provisions"* relating to the establishment of the new administration. Section 21 provided: The Congress shall provide efficacious procedures and adequate remedies for the reversion to the State of all lands of the public domain and real rights connected therewith which were acquired in violation of the Constitution or the public land laws, or through corrupt practices. No transfer or disposition of such lands or real rights shall be allowed until after the lapse of one year from the ratification of this Constitution.

Initial steps towards land reform were covered in Section 22, which specified: At the earliest possible time, the government shall expropriate idle or abandoned agricultural lands as may be defined by law, for distribution to the beneficiaries of the agrarian reform program.

Sections 24 and 25 covered private armies and foreign bases respectively. 24. Private armies and other armed groups not recognized by duly constituted authority shall be dismantled. All paramilitary forces including Civilian Home Defense Forces not consistent with the citizen armed force established in this Constitution, shall be dissolved or, where appropriate, converted into the regular force.

25. After the expiration in 1991 of the Agreement between the Republic of the Philippines and the United States of America concerning Military Bases, foreign military bases, troops, or facilities shall not be allowed in

the Philippines except under a treaty duly concurred in by the Senate and, when the Congress so requires, ratified by a majority of the votes cast by the people in a national referendum held for that purpose, and recognized as a treaty by the other contracting State.

Section 26 outlined the new government's powers to seize assets of former "Marcos cronies".

26. The authority to issue sequestration or freeze orders under Proclamation No. 3 dated March 25, 1986 in relation to the recovery of ill-gotten wealth shall remain operative for not more than eighteen months after the ratification of this Constitution. However, in the national interest, as certified by the President, the Congress may extend said period. A sequestration or freeze order shall be issued only upon showing of a prima facie case. The order and the list of the sequestered or frozen properties shall forthwith be registered with the proper court. For orders issued before the ratification of this Constitution, the correspond-ing judicial action or proceeding shall be filed within six months from its ratification. For those issued after such ratification, the judicial action or proceeding shall be commenced within six months from the issuance thereof. The sequestration or freeze order is deemed automatically lifted if no judicial action or proceeding is commenced as herein provided.

POLITICAL STRUCTURE

THE GOVERNMENT

Head of state

Mrs Corazon Aquino	President
Mr Salvador Laurel	Vice-President

Members of the Cabinet

Gen. Fidel Famos	Defence
Mr Sedfrey Ordonez	Justice
Mr Vincente Jayme	Finance
Mr Catalino Macaraig	Executive Secretary
Mr Raul Manglapus	Acting Secretary for Foreign Affairs
Mr Juanito Ferrer	Local Government
Mr Fiorello Estuar	Public Works and Highways
Mr Jose Concepcion	Trade and Industry
Mr Carlos Dominguez	Agriculture
Mr Ramon Diaz	Presidential Commission on Good Government
Mr Luis Villafuerte	Presidential Commission on Government Reorganization
Mr Jose Antonio Gonzales	Tourism
Mr Antonio Arizabal	Science and Technology
Dr Lourdes Quisumbing	Education, Culture and Sport
Mr Fulgencio Factoran	Natural Resources
Mr Guillermo Carague	Budget
Mr Franklin Drilon	Labour and Employment
Mr Mamita Pardo de Tavera	Social Services and Development
Mr Alfredo R. A. Bengzon	Health
Mr Reinerio Reyes	Transport and Communications
Mr Teodoro Benigno	Press Secretary
Ms Solita Monsod	Director General of National Economic and Development Authority
Mr Jose Fernandez	Governor of Central Bank

THE ARMED FORCES

The total strength of the armed forces of the Philippines is 113,000. Recruitment is voluntary. Total reserves number 48,000 (Army 20,000; Navy 12,000; Air Force 16,000). The Army has 70,000 personnel, divided into five infantry divisions, one ranger regiment, two engineer brigades, one light armed regiment, four artillery regiments, one military police brigade and the Presidential Security Command. The Navy has 26,000 personnel, including 9,500 Marines and 2,000 Coastguard. It has seven frigates, 10 corvettes, 86 patrol craft and a number of auxiliary vessels and amphibious units. The Coastguard has 65 patrol craft, with additional craft on order. The Air Force has 17,000 personnel with four main combat squadrons, one helicopter wing and various transport and training units. Official paramilitary forces include 42,000 under the Ministry of Defence, and 50,000 in the Philippines Constabulary. There are also an uncertain number of unofficial or semi-official vigilante groups, which in some areas work closely with the local army command.

TRADE UNIONS

Trade unions were first legalized in 1908 and the first labour congress was held in 1913. Following the declaration of martial law by Marcos in 1972 (when many trade union leaders were dismissed) the labour code was revised in 1974 to curb the right to strike and to bring about the unification of the labour movement, leading to the formation of the Trade Union Congress of the Philippines (TUCP). The principal limitations on strike action in force in 1985 included: (i) a wide range of circumstances in which the government could on the grounds of the national interest ban a strike, impose compulsory arbitration, and bring about the dismissal and imprisonment for up to six months of strikers; (ii) the possible permanent deportation of foreign workers participating in an illegal strike; (iii) sentences of penal servitude for life for organizers of pickets or other collective actions held to be meetings or demonstrations used for anti-government propaganda purposes, and lesser sentences of imprisonment for participants in such actions; and (iv) the requirment of the approval of a two-thirds majority of workers in a margaining unit for a strike to be called. (In practice, however, strikes in various public interest sectors had occurred without prosecutions, although compulsory arbitration was used to end 33 strikes in 1983.) The incoming Aquino government in 1986 announced that it would amend the existing labour legislation so as to remove restrictions on strike action and to extend the right to organize and collective bargaining (guaranteed by the 1974 labour code to private sector industrial, commercial and agricultural workers) to workers in the civil service and government-owned or controlled corporations. There were 1,960 registered trade unions in 1985, with a

REVOLUTION IN THE PHILIPPINES?

total of 4,780,000 members (this figure including, however, 2,670,000 peasant farmers). There were 366 strikes, involving 102,000 workers, in 1985, and 490 strikes in the first nine months of 1986.

The Philippines ratified ILO Convention No. 87 (Freedom of Association and Protection of the Right to Organize, 1948) in 1957 and Convention No. 98 (Right to Organize and Collective Bargaining, 1949) in 1953.

The Federation of Free Workers (FFW), which claims some 400,000 members, was founded in 1950 and developed with the assistance of the Roman Catholic clergy. Its president is Juan C. Tan, who is also president of the Brussels-based World Confederation of Labour. At its 16th national convention, held in April 1986, the FFW called for: (i) the right to form unions to be extended to public employees; (ii) full rights to strike and picket; (iii) the promotion of conciliation, mediation and voluntary arbitration and the ending of compulsory arbitration; (iv) restraints on the use of injunctions in labour disputes; (v) removal of barriers to union registration, and the lowering of the requirement that 30 per cent of workers in any bargaining unit must join a union for it to be registered; and (vi) the abolition of clauses in the labour code structuring trade unions on a one-industry, one federation basis. The FFW favours a managed, co-operative economy, with profit-sharing and extended social benefits. *International affiliation.* WCL.

The leftist-orientated May First Movement or Kilusang Mayo Uno (KMU), now led by Crispin Beltran, was formed in 1983 and claims 500,000 members; it has been prominent in industrial militancy, and is regarded as a communist front by the military. Rolando Olalia, the previous national chairman of the union and also formerly chairman of the newly-formed People's Party (Partido Ng Bayan—PNB), was found brutally murdered on November 13, 1986, and party leaders attributed his killing to forces within the military. The KMU had on November 12 stated that it would call a general strike in the event of a military coup (which was widely expected at the time) to overthrow the Aquino government; the union had boycotted the February 1986 elections which brought Aquino to power, but had subsequently given support to the new government while calling for fundamental reforms.

An independent federation of small farmers, the Peasant Movement, led by Jaime Tadeo, has about 700,000 members.

The Philippine Congress of Trade Unions (PHILCONTU) has 34 affiliated organizations and a total of 1,200,000 members.

The Philippines Trade Union Council (PTUC), founded in 1954 and led by Aurelio Intertas (president) and Gabrial Gatchalian (general secretary), has 10 affiliated federations and a total of nearly 300,000 members. It is affiliated to the International Congress of Free Trade Unions.

POLITICAL STRUCTURE

The Trade Union Congress of the Philippines (TUCP) is the largest trade union centre in the Philippines, with some 4,000,000 members including the National Congress of Farmers' Organizations with which it has a solidarity pact. It includes a number of autonomous general federations. Its president is Democrito Mendoza and its general secretary Ernesto Herrera. It was formed in 1975 in response to the implementation of the 1974 labour code which emphasized the co-ordination and unification of the trade union movement, reflecting the official view of President Marcos that such unification would both benefit the labour movement and provide a favourable environment for economic development. According to some sections of organized labour the TUCP had been unduly close to the Marcos government; it did, however, mobilize 7,000 volunteers for the watchdog National Citizens' Movement for Free Elections (NAMFREL) which unofficially supervised the February 1986 election. The TUCP's policies as defined in mid-1986 included the extension of collective bargaining to government-owned or controlled corporations and to managerial employees; expanded conciliation and mediation and the creation of a full-time arbitration body; an end to the dominance of government on tripartite agencies; the reorganization and reform of the National Wages Council; an end to restrictions on strikes; and measures to relieve unemployment and under-employment. It has no political affiliation, and emphasizes the improvement of industrial relations.

Under the Aquino regime, the TUCP continued to offer broad support to the government, thereby perpetuating the rift between it and other labour organizations, many of whom it portrays as "communist fronts". It favours a "non-adversarial" approach to industrial disputes and supports the government's "tripartite" approach to labour relations by participating in committees composed jointly of government, employers and union representatives.

The TUCP has 35 affiliated unions, including the Associated Labor Unions (ALU-PHILCONTU); the Association of Trade Unions; the Confederation of Labor and Allied Social Services; Federation of Free Farmers; the Federation of Filipino Civilian Employees Association; the Federation of Agrarian and Industrial Toiling Hands; the National Association of Free Trade Unions; the National Labor Unions; the National Congress of Unions in the Sugar Industry of the Philippines; the Grand Labor Union; the Philippine Federation of Labor; the Philippine Association of Free Trade Unions (PAFLU-SEPTEMBER); the Philippine Labor Federation; the Philippines Labor Unity Movement—Federation of Industrial and Agrarian Workers (PLUM); the Philippine Technical, Clerical and Commercial Employees Association; the Philippine Government Employees Association; and the Workers Alliance of Trade Unions.

WOMEN'S MOVEMENTS

According to figures issued by the National Census and Statistics Office 1986, 48.5 per cent of women are economically active, with 19 per cent of women workers being employed in services, 13 per cent in agriculture, and 5 per cent in industry. More detailed figures issued in 1983 showed women making up 63 per cent of professional and technical workers; 50 per cent of clerical workers; 66 per cent of sales workers; 61 per cent of service workers; 25 per cent of administrative workers; 30 per cent of agricultural workers; and 23 per cent of production and related workers. In 1985, GABRIELA (see below) reported that a study showed women earning only between 31 and 41 per cent of that earned by their male counterparts. The Philippines ratified ILO Convention No. 100 (Equal Remuneration, 1951) in 1953 and No. 111 (Discrimination—Employment and Occupation, 1958) in 1960.

Women are prohibited from acquiring personal property without their husband's consent, although they may benefit through familial inheritance. Abortion is illegal, and reports indicate that back-street and self-induced abortions are common, accounting for the majority of maternal deaths in the country. Contraceptive services have customarily been inaccessible to the majority of the rural population. The poverty of most Filipino women combined with the importance of tourism to the national economy had encouraged widespread prostitution and the sale of "mail order brides" abroad.

The General Assembly Binding Women for Reforms, Integrity, Equality, Leadership and Action (GABRIELA) is a militant, progressive and nationalist grouping of over 100 organizations, institutions and programmes representing approximately 30,000 members (women only). Its activities include income-generating and community development programmes; campaigning and lobbying for women's rights and support systems (issues addressed include maternal health-care facilities, maternity benefits, contraception and abortion rights); vocational training and educational programmes; the development of feminist research; and protest campaigns against sexual harassment and gender-based discrimination, prostitution, female boxing, militarization and the presence of US bases. The formation of GABRIELA was inspired by an all-women's march organized by SAMAKANA (an organization for housewives) on October 28, 1983, to protest against the Marcos regime.

In October 1986 AMIHAN, the National Federation of Peasant Women, was launched with the aid of GABRIELA after a series of consultations with representatives of 11 peasant women's organizations already existing in different parts of the country. The Federation is now composed of 24 member organizations and it has a membership of some 8,000 women. Since its inception, it had protested against the massacre of farmer demonstrators and what it sees as the failure of the Aquino government to implement a genuine land reform programme. It has also campaigned against a government plan to limit support for family planning programmes.

Women for the Motherland, founded in October 1986, is the first all-women political party in the Philippines. It plans to put up women candidates for all elections and is currently screening potential candidates. Its prime campaigning interests include education, health, housing, reduction of the military and the need for more special services for women.

RELIGION

Around 90 per cent of Filipinos profess adherence to Christianity, of whom the vast majority are Roman Catholics. Moslems predominate in large areas of Mindanao, and are also represented in areas of Manila and on other islands. There is a small Buddhist community, while Animist beliefs survive in some more remote areas, and continue to exert an influence over both Christians and Moslems.

The Roman Catholic community is organized into 16 archdioceses and 47 dioceses. The non-Roman Christian churches include the Church of Christ; the Convention of Philippine Baptist Churches, the Lutherans; the Philippine Independent Church; the Union Church of Manila; and the United Church of Christ.

REFERENCES AND SOURCES

In addition to the sources listed below, much valuable information has been obtained directly from many of the organizations listed in the reference section.

Embassy of the Philippines, London: 9a Palace Green, London, W8 4QE. Tel. 01-937-1609.

National Census and Statistics Office, Manila.

National Economic and Development Authority, Manila.

Philippines Central Bank Statistical Report.

Philippines Central Bank Report, 1986.

Philippine Yearbook.

FAO Production Yearbook.

Keesings Reference Publications, all published by Longman Group UK Limited:

Keesing's Record of World Events.

People in Power.

Revolutionary and Dissident Movements (1988).

Political Parties of the World, 3rd Ed. (1988).

Border and Territorial Disputes, 2nd Ed. (1987).

Trade Unions of the World (1987).

State Economic Agencies of the World (1985).

Treaties and Alliances of the World, 4th Ed. (1986).

Women's Movements of the World (1988).

Communist and Marxist Parties of the World (1986).

Among other sources containing information on the Philippines, the following deserve particular recommendation:

Far Eastern Economic Review (Review Publishing Company Ltd., Hong Kong)

Asia Yearbook (Review Publishing Company Ltd., Hong Kong)

Economist Intelligence Unit (publishes quarterly and annual reports on the Philippines).

Europa Yearbook (Europa Publications).

INDEX

INDEX

INDEX

INDEX

"Sparrow squads", 18; 60; 61; 63-4; 86
"Strategic hamlets", 15; 18
Subic Bay naval base, 7; 80-2
Sugar industry, 3; 69; 71; 75-77; 84

T

Tadeo, Jaime, 44
Tanada, Lorenzo, 21
Tanada, Wigberto, 81
Tapia, Maj.-Gen. Cesar, 67
Task Force on Detainees, 28
Thailand, 82
Tiwark ("Upside Down"), 38
Tolentino, Arturo, 20; 30; 32; 33; 45
Tourism, 86-87; 89; 90
Trade unions, 12; 23; 34; 52; 73
Treaty of Paris, 4
Tripoli agreement, 14; 22; 41; 67

United Kingdom, 3
United States:
Aid, 6; 79; 80
Marcos, 8; 19; 23-6; 31; 36; 50
Military bases, 5; 7; 13; 17; 19; 22; 40;
58; 63; 64; 80-3
Regional policy, 3-9; 13; 16; 19; 23-6;
55; 79-83

V

Vargas, Jose, 5
Ver, Gen. Fabian, 18; 26; 32; 32; 71
Vigilantes, 51; 61; 62; 67; 76; 89

W

World Anti-Communist League, 51; 80
World Bank, 77

U

Unemployment, 72
Unido (United Nationalist Democratic
Organization), 16; 17; 19; 20-22; 27;
45; 46
United Association of Transport
Workers (UATW), 52
United Democratic Opposition, 16

Y

Yamashita, Gen. Tomoyuki, 51

Z

Zumel, Antonio, 38; 40
Zumel, Brig.-Gen. Jose Maria, 32; 36

150